CW01189447

CUTTING EDGE

THIRD EDITION

INTERMEDIATE

WORKBOOK

WITH KEY

JANE COMYNS CARR FRANCES EALES
AND DAMIAN WILLIAMS

CONTENTS

01 YOUR WORLD

Language focus 1
Questions and short answers

1 Put the words in the correct order to make questions.

1 London / first / your / to / Is / visit / this ?
Is this your first visit to London?
2 your / is / going / How / job ?
______
3 here / When / you / did / get ?
______
4 all / family / is / your / How ?
______
5 do / do / you / How ?
______
6 journey / you / here / a / good / Did / have ?
______
7 things / you / How / are / with ?
______
8 staying / you / are / Where / while / here / you / are ?
______

2 Complete the questions in the conversation with the correct form of *be*, *have* or *do*.

A: What [1] *'s* your girlfriend's name?
B: Masako.
A: [2] ______ that a Japanese name?
B: Yes, that's right.
A: Which part of Japan [3] ______ she come from?
B: Osaka.
A: Uh-huh ... so [4] ______ you speak Japanese?
B: No. 'Hello' and 'thank you', but that's it!
A: Oh, right. [5] ______ she doing that English course with you last month?
B: No, her English is much better than mine.
A: Well, how [6] ______ you meet her, then?
B: At the bus stop – she lives near me.
A: I see. [7] ______ she got her own flat here?
B: Well, it's her parents' flat.
A: Oh. [8] ______ they living here, too?
B: Some of the time, yes.

3a Match questions 1–10 with short answers a–j below.

1 Do you like our new teacher? [g]
2 Have you got the time? [ ]
3 Is it cold outside today? [ ]
4 Did you have a good holiday? [ ]
5 Was there a lot of traffic on the roads this morning? [ ]
6 Are your neighbours nice? [ ]
7 Were you at the football match on Saturday? [ ]
8 Has your brother got a girlfriend? [ ]
9 Does it take long to do this exercise? [ ]
10 Was the film good? [ ]

a Yes, they are.
b No, he hasn't.
c Yes, I did.
d Yes, I was.
e No, it wasn't.
f No, it isn't.
g ~~Yes, I do.~~
h No, it doesn't.
i Yes, there was.
j No, I haven't.

b 1.1 Listen to the questions and answers. Notice that the auxiliaries *do/does*, *has/have*, *is/are* and *was/were* are weak in the questions, but strong in the short answers.

/ də /
A: Do you like our new teacher?
/ du: /
B: Yes, I do.

c Listen again and repeat the questions and answers, paying attention to the strong and weak sounds.

4 Look at the answers. Write the question for each one.

1 *What's your full name ?*
Mark Thomas Williams.
2 ______
Yes, I do. I live with my family.
3 ______
They're looking at page 7.
4 ______
He lives in the centre of town, opposite the cinema.
5 ______
My holiday was great, thanks. We had lovely weather and food.
6 ______
I usually get up around 8 o'clock.
7 ______
No, she doesn't. My English teacher doesn't speak my language.
8 ______
I went to university in New York.

5 Find and correct the mistakes in questions 1–9.

1 How to pronounce 'b-u-s-i-n-e-s-s'?
How do you pronounce 'b-u-s-i-n-e-s-s'
2 Can you writing 'customer' on the board, please?
______
3 What's English word for this?
______
4 Which page we are on?
______
5 Have anybody got a spare pen?
______
6 Can you say again that, please?
______
7 What are tonight's homework?
______
8 How you spell 'journey'?
______
9 What means 'colleague'?
______

Pronunciation
Sentence stress in questions

6a Underline the stressed words in the questions and short answers below.

1 Where exactly do you live?
2 How do you spell your name?
3 Have you got any brothers and sisters?
4 No, I haven't.
5 Which one would you like?
6 Does your mother speak English?
7 Yes, actually she does.
8 How was your weekend?
9 What's your date of birth?
10 What time do you usually get up in the morning?

b 1.2 Listen and check. Practise saying the questions.

Vocabulary
People around you

7 Add letters to complete the words.

1 n *i* *e* c *e*
2 p _ r _ _ t
3 _ _ l _ t _ v _
4 _ t _ a _ g _ _
5 c _ u _ i _
6 a _ q _ a _ _ t _ n _ _
7 c _ a _ _ m _ t _
8 _ o _ _ e _ g _ e
9 s _ e _ m _ t _ e _
10 n _ i _ h _ _ _ r

Language focus 2

Present simple and Present continuous

8a Read the three extracts A–C below. Which is from:

1 a detective story? ______
2 an encyclopaedia? ______
3 an email to a pen friend? ______

b Complete the extracts with the Present simple form of the verbs in the boxes.

A

~~live~~ do (x3) help look own rain

New Message

We [1] *live* in Lisbon. My parents [2]________ a furniture shop, and I [3]________ them in the shop at weekends. Please write back and tell me about you and your family.

What [4]________ you ________ like? (Can you send a photo?) What [5]________ your parents ________? And what about the weather in England? [6]________ it really ________ all the time?

B

believe belong not know own want know

So who [7]________ the gun ________ to, Smith?' 'Well, Inspector, we [8]________ that only three people in the village [9]________ a gun, but we [10]________ which of them had a motive for killing the Professor. Let's go back to the scene of the crime – I [11]________ to try an experiment. [12]________ you ________ in telepathy, Inspector Turner?

C

come get not drink have not have spend

INFOPEDIA
THE FREE ENCYCLOPEDIA

Koala

The koala is an Australian mammal. It [13]________ thick fur and round ears but it [14]________ a tail, like a teddy bear. Koalas [15]________ most of the day sleeping. They [16]________ water, but they [17]________ liquids from eating eucalyptus leaves. The word *koala* [18]________ from the Aborigine word meaning 'no drink'.

9 Complete the sentences with the Present continuous form of the verbs in the box.

~~visit~~ breathe clean die eat get (x2) have not get not set spend stay suffer talk use watch

'This is Sandra Wise with the news headlines: the president [1] *is visiting* the UK this week. He and his wife [2]________ at London's famous Savoy Hotel. Today he [3]________ a meeting with the British prime minister, and later in the week ...'
'... later on Ten News Tonight: why we as a nation [4]________ fat. A nutrition expert says that our children [5]________ too much junk food and [6]________ enough exercise, and as parents we [7]________ a good example: we [8]________ more time than ever in the car or in front of the TV ...'
'... and finally, [9]________ your health ________ because of indoor pollution? [10]________ you ________ in dangerous chemicals while you sit at home watching this programme? According to a report by the Clean Air Society, this is a serious problem for millions of people. The president of the society even claims that people [11]________ because of the air they breathe in their own homes.'

A: Hi, Robin, it's Kris. [12]________ you ________ the news on TV?
B: No, actually I [13]________ the kitchen! I [14]________ ready for Sammy's party tomorrow.
A: [15]________ you ________ a cleaner with chemicals in it?
B: Well, yes, I suppose. Kris, what [16]________ you ________ about?
A: Oh, it's just that there was an item about indoor pollution, and ...

10 **Complete the conversation with the Present simple or continuous form of the verbs in brackets.**

A: How can I help you, Mr Daniels?

B: Well, I started having bad headaches a couple of weeks ago and they [1] *'re getting* (get) worse. I can't sleep, I'm tired all the time, and the worst thing is my hair [2] ______ (go) grey and I'm only 31!

A: I see. Let me ask you some questions. [3] ______ (you smoke)?

B: No, I gave up a month ago.

A: Right. I see you're a salesman. How many hours a week [4] ______ (you work)?

B: Well, I normally [5] ______ (do) eight hours a day, but at the moment I [6] ______ (work) at least ten hours and some Saturdays.

A: That is a lot. How [7] ______ (you relax)?

B: Well, I usually [8] ______ (sit) in front of the TV with a pizza and a few beers.

A: Hmm. [9] ______ (you do) any exercise at the moment?

B: Not really, but I'm losing a lot of weight and I [10] ______ (not know) why.

A: I think you [11] ______ (suffer) from stress. I [12] ______ (want) you to eat a more varied diet and to do some exercise. Come back and see me in four weeks and I'll check you again.

Listen and read

Ordinary heroes

11a 1.3 **A TV station is doing some research for a programme about ordinary people who are considered 'heroes' by people around them. Listen and read the emails and answer the questions.**

Whose hero is:

1 a stranger? ______
2 a relative? ______
3 a colleague? ______

b **Listen and read again and answer the questions.**

Who:

1 is very brave? ______
2 nearly left her job? ______
3 nearly lost a lot of money? ______
4 was terrified of her boss? ______
5 is in a lot of pain? ______
6 told his boss what he thought of him? ______
7 is more generous than many adults? ______
8 wants to contact his/her hero? ______

New Message

My 'hero' at the moment is Ricky.

We work together. I was thinking of leaving the place where I work because of our horrible new boss. He's always in a bad mood and he never has a good word to say to anyone. He also picks on young female members of staff: there's a girl called Kimberley who's terrified of him. Or at least she was. When Ricky joined us, everything changed. First he covered for me when I was late back from lunch by telling the boss that I was downstairs in the photocopying room.

Then a couple of days later, the boss was standing at Kimberley's desk, shouting at her, telling her she was lazy and would have to stay late to finish her work ... Anyway, Ricky marched straight up to him and told him he was a pathetic coward for talking to his staff like that. Well, the boss was stunned to silence – he just walked off without saying another word and he's left us alone since then.

Charlotte, Bristol

New Message

I'm writing to tell you about my niece, Mary.

She's only seven and she's in hospital at the moment. She was in a bad car accident two weeks ago and she broke both her legs. She's had one operation and now she's waiting for another, then she'll have to be in a wheelchair for quite a while. Anyway, I am constantly amazed by this little girl's courage: she never cries when she has an injection, and very rarely complains about the considerable pain that she must be in.

When I go in to visit her, she always has a smile for me, and last time I went she was comforting another girl who was upset because her parents couldn't come and visit her. I've also noticed that she shares all the chocolates and toys that people have given her with the other children in her ward. I don't know how many adults would be as generous as that!

Dan, Newcastle

New Message

I'm hoping that by writing to you, I might be able to get in touch with my 'hero' again.

I don't know him – I don't even know his name – but what he did was unbelievably kind and honest. I went shopping at my local supermarket last Friday, and I met an old friend at the checkout desk. We chatted for a while, then I loaded up the car and came home.

It was only then that I realised I'd lost my purse: I thought maybe I'd dropped it in the car park. I started to panic when I also remembered that I had quite a lot of money in it. Then someone knocked at the door and it was a complete stranger, holding out my purse! He said he was in the queue behind me at the supermarket checkout and that's where he found my purse. He got my address from my driving licence. I was so grateful, but I didn't know what to say.

Anyway, he just walked off, and I haven't been able to thank him properly.

Annette, Leeds

Vocabulary
Everyday activities

12 Match questions 1–10 with answers a–j. Then complete the sentences with the words/phrases in the box.

~~go to the gym~~ looking after children commuting playing video games texting going on social networking sites doing paperwork going shopping tidying up doing nothing

1 Have you lost weight? You look amazing! c
2 Do you enjoy being a teacher?
3 I'm really nervous about the exam next week.
4 We have a cleaner who comes in once a week.
5 I haven't seen Luc and Sophie for weeks, have you?
6 What do you like doing at the weekend?
7 Why was your computer so expensive?
8 Are you happy you moved to the countryside?
9 Oh no, my phone bill is huge!
10 Are you looking forward to your holiday?

a I wish we had someone like that. I hate ________________ !
b Oh yes, it's much quieter here, but I do spend a lot of time ________________ to work.
c Thanks! I *go to the gym* three times a week.
d I love ________________ with my friends and buying new clothes.
e Oh yes. Three weeks of lying on the beach and ________________ . I can't wait!
f If you spend less time ________________ and more time studying, I'm sure you'll be fine.
g You shouldn't do so much ________________ . It's cheaper and you can say more by calling.
h It needs to be powerful because I like ________________ on it.
i Well, I love being in the classroom but I don't like all the administration – I hate ________________ .
j No, now that they're parents they spend most of their time ________________ .

Writing
An informal email

13a Read Grace's reply to an email from Katarina. In which paragraph does she do the following?

a Write about her own news. *2*
b Respond to Katarina's news. ______
c Respond to Katarina's request. ______

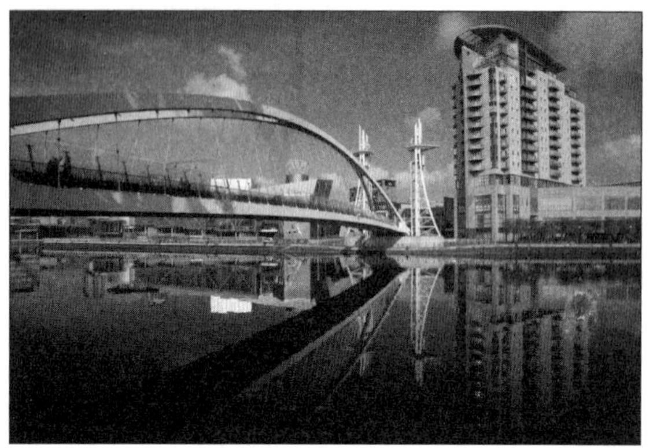

Re: A message from Katarina

Hi Katarina!

[1]What a lovely surprise to get your message! Of course I remember you – how could I forget? It was great to hear all your news. You look great in your photos, you haven't changed a bit. I loved looking at them and remembering all the times we had together. I'm pleased that you're happy in Bratislava, and Hendrik looks really nice, too. You must tell me all about him! Your job sounds really interesting, I always knew you would end up doing something exciting. I miss our time at university, too. It was such fun!

[2]As for my news, well, I'm also very busy these days. I'm still in Manchester and I'm working as an English teacher in a private language school. The job's stressful, but I really love it as I meet people from all over the world. I'm married now to a guy I met at work called Jack. We've got a little girl called Charlotte (but everyone calls her Charlie), who is lovely but a bit naughty at times! It's funny that you asked about Tom. He finished his studies, then decided he didn't want to be a lawyer and went travelling round the world! I think he's in Thailand at the moment, but we don't hear from him very often. As for my parents, mum retired a few years ago and dad retired last year, and now they spend a lot of time in the garden. They both seem very happy.

[3]It was great to hear that you're coming to Manchester next week. It would be fantastic to see you again, and I can't wait to meet Hendrik! I want you to meet Jack and Charlie too, and we can catch up on all our news. Let me know which days you are going to be here and we can plan something special.

Great to hear from you.
Take care, and lots of love,

Grace

b Write the phrases from the email that Grace uses to do the following.

1 respond to getting Katarina's message
What a lovely surprise to get your message!
2 say that she remembers Katarina
______
3 respond to hearing Katarina's news
______
4 comment on Katarina's photos
______
5 ask about Hendrik
______
6 introduce her own news
______
7 introduce her news about Tom
______
8 introduce her news about her parents
______
9 say how she feels about seeing Katarina again
______
10 say how she felt about receiving Katarina's message
______

c Look at the information below. You have received a message from an old friend, Dan. Write a reply using some of the phrases you have learnt from exercise 13b and tell him your news.

Dan's news
- He moved to New York after university.
- He got married to Maria, and has two children, Sam and Ben.
- He's working as a journalist for a large national newspaper as a business correspondent.
- He's very busy but loves his job.

Dan's request
- They're coming to your town for a week next month (alone).
- Can they stay with you?

Language live
Keeping a conversation going

14a Choose the correct answers to complete the conversations.

1 **A:** I'm working in advertising at the moment. [b]
B: *Do you?* / *Are you?* (circled: *Are you?*)
2 **A:** I don't get on very well with my brother. [ ]
B: *Don't you?* / *Do you?*
3 **A:** I've never seen the sea. [ ]
B: *Have you?* / *Haven't you?*
4 **A:** We once shared a flat together. [ ]
B: *Did you?* / *Were you?*
5 **A:** I'm thinking of going to Spain this year. [ ]
B: *Were you?* / *Are you?*
6 **A:** Our class was really interesting today. [ ]
B: *Was it?* / *Was she?*
7 **A:** Annika went skiing last month. [ ]
B: *Did she?* / *Was she?*
8 **A:** Dave and I both have the same surname. [ ]
B: *Do they?* / *Do you?*

b Match phrases a–h below to conversations 1–8 in exercise 14a.

a Why's that then? [2]
b That sounds interesting. [ ]
c What a coincidence! [ ]
d When was that? [ ]
e That sounds fun. [ ]
f That's amazing! [ ]
g What did you do? [ ]
h Where exactly? [ ]

c 🎧 1.4 Listen and check. Practise saying the questions using the same intonation.

02 MEMORY

Language focus 1

Past simple and Past continuous

1 **Complete the conversations with the Past simple form of the verbs in the box.**

~~not see~~	cook	forget	get (x2)	go	happen
hear	introduce		rain	ring	stay
not tell	not want				

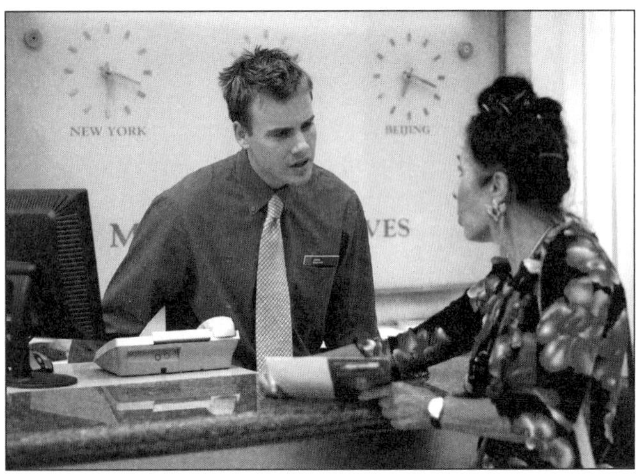

A **A:** Oh sorry, I [1] *didn't see* you there. [2]__________ you __________ the bell?
B: No, I [3]__________ to disturb you.

B **A:** [4]__________ you __________ out last night?
B: No, actually we [5]__________ in and Gary [6]__________ a fantastic meal.

C **A:** [7]__________ you __________ about Abby and Rob's disastrous holiday?
B: No, what [8]__________ ?
A: Well, the weather was terrible – it [9]__________ every day, and they both [10]__________ food poisoning from the hotel food!

D **A:** Why [11]__________ you __________ me about Marc's engagement? I [12]__________ quite a shock when he [13]__________ me to his fiancée.
B: Oh, I'm so sorry. I [14]__________ to tell you. She's nice, isn't she?

2 **Complete the sentences with the Past continuous form of the verbs in brackets.**

1 I'm sorry I'm late, I *was waiting* (wait) for the babysitter.
2 Who __________ (you talk) to on the phone just now?
3 Sorry, I __________ (not concentrate) – can you explain that again, please?
4 **A:** I saw Lee in the jewellery store on Saturday.
B: Oh! What __________ (he do)?
A: Well, he __________ (buy) a diamond ring!
5 **A:** How do you work this thing again?
B: No idea! I __________ (not listen) when he explained it to us.
6 **A:** Why wasn't Mia at work yesterday?
B: I think she __________ (move) house.
7 I saw Renée with her new boyfriend yesterday. They __________ (have) an argument.
8 Sorry, __________ (we make) a lot of noise? We __________ (put) up some shelves.

3 **Choose a phrase from each box to make a complete answer for questions 1–6 below.**

~~I was peeling some onions and~~
She was travelling home from work and she
We were sunbathing at the weekend and we
They were staying in Florida when
He was walking in the rain and he
He was playing football and he

got very wet.
stayed out too long.
~~the knife slipped.~~
left it on the bus.
fell over.
there was a terrible storm.

1 How did you cut your finger?
I was peeling some onions and the knife slipped.
2 How did Tony hurt his knee?
____
3 How did you all get so sunburnt?
____
4 How did Martin catch a cold?
____
5 How did a tree fall on the Simpson's car?
____
6 How did Sarah lose her bag?
____

4 Complete the conversations with the correct form of the verbs in brackets.

A **A:** I phoned you last night at 8 p.m. but you didn't answer. What [1] *were you doing* (you do)?

B: I [2] ________________ (work) on my computer and I [3] ________________ (not hear) the phone ring.

B **A:** Good morning. ICI. May I help you?

B: Hello, yes. I [4] ________________ (talk) to the financial director a minute ago and the line [5] ________________ (go) dead.

A: Oh, I'm sorry, madam. I'll reconnect you.

C **A:** When did you meet your husband?

B: When I [6] ________________ (be) in Canada four years ago.

A: Were you on holiday?

B: No, I [7] ________________ (train) to be a ski instructor, but I [8] ________________ (break) my leg. I [9] ________________ (spend) eight weeks in hospital and he was my doctor!

5 Use the prompts to make two conversations about accidents.

A **A:** Penny told me you / have / accident yesterday. What / happen?

[1] *Penny told me you had an accident yesterday. What happened?*

B: We / drive / home and another car / stop / suddenly and we / crash / into the back of it.

[2] ________________

A: Be / the other car all right?

[3] ________________

B: Yes, luckily we / not go / very fast.

[4] ________________

B **A:** What / you / do to your hand?

[5] ________________

B: I / burn / it.

[6] ________________

A: Oh no, how?

B: I / iron / a shirt, and the phone / ring, and I / put / the iron down on my hand by mistake!

[7] ________________

Pronunciation

Past simple *-ed* endings

6a How many syllables do these *-ed* forms have? Mark the stressed syllables • and the unstressed syllables ◦.

1	hàppened (• ◦)	2	**8**	changed	☐
2	stopped	☐	**9**	practised	☐
3	travelled	☐	**10**	opened	☐
4	looked	☐	**11**	improved	☐
5	reminded	☐	**12**	received	☐
6	visited	☐	**13**	repeated	☐
7	phoned	☐	**14**	answered	☐

b 2.1 Listen to the verbs in phrases and repeat them.

Vocabulary

Childhood and upbringing

7 Complete the sentences with the correct form of the words/phrases in the box.

~~ashamed~~ strict tell off give confidence encourage pocket money get into trouble argue respect punish praise

1 I once stole my sister's toy and my parents found out. I felt really *ashamed*.

2 Children today don't ________________ their parents enough, I think. They're often rude to them.

3 When I was younger, my parents always ________________ me to do well at school.

4 My parents never gave me any ________________. I had to earn my own money.

5 I once ________________ for not doing my homework. My parents ________________ me by not letting me go out with my friends.

6 Whenever I did well at school, my parents ________________ me a lot, which ________________ me a lot of ________________.

7 If I ________________ with my brother, my parents would ________________ us ________________.

8 My parents were very ________________. I wasn't allowed to see my friends in the week and I had to go to bed at 8 p.m.

Language focus 2
used to and *would*

8 Cross out any unnecessary words in the sentences below. Where necessary, replace the main verb with the auxiliary *do*.

1 I used to have long hair but I don't ~~have long hair~~ anymore.
2 My friends and I didn't use to go to the gym every week, but now we go to the gym every week.
3 My boyfriend used to be a terrible cook, but he isn't a terrible cook any more.
4 There used to be a lot of traffic in my city, and there still is a lot of traffic.
5 I didn't use to know how to send text messages, but now I know how to send text messages.
6 When I was younger, I would spend a lot of time reading, but now I don't spend a lot of time reading.
7 I didn't use to like spiders and I still don't like spiders!
8 My family didn't use to go overseas for our holidays, but now we go overseas for our holidays.
9 I used to be very shy but I'm not shy any longer.
10 In my old job, I would often stay in the office late, but now I don't stay in the office late.

9a Look at the pictures and notes about Virginia's life ten years ago and now. Write eight sentences about how her life has changed, using *used to* and *didn't use to*.

1 *She used to live in England.*
2 ______
3 ______
4 ______
5 ______
6 ______
7 ______
8 ______

b Now write eight sentences using *still* and *not … anymore / any longer*.

1 *She still wears fashionable clothes.*
2 *She doesn't live in England anymore.*
3 ______
4 ______
5 ______
6 ______
7 ______
8 ______

Listen and read

I used to believe

10a 2.2 Listen and read the extracts from a website where people write about their childhood beliefs. Which stories are shown in pictures A–D?

A ☐

B ☐

C ☐

D ☐

b Match extracts 1–10 with the topics below.

time	3
language	☐
animals	☐
transport	☐
countries	☐
politics	☐
drink	☐
food	☐
teachers	☐
kitchen appliances	☐

I used to believe

1 'I used to believe that countries really had their names written across them and that when you reached a border there would be red dotted lines on the ground.'

2 'I used to think that the trails that aeroplanes leave across the sky are created by the pilots leaning out of the windows holding a piece of chalk, so they know where they've been. That's what I was told, anyway.'

3 'I used to have problems when I was trying to learn how to read a real clock. My theory was that if an hour is longer than a minute, then the long hand was the hour and the short hand was for minutes. I was always late coming home … or really early.'

4 'I remember I used to be very scared of swallowing seeds when I was small. Once when I swallowed a lemon pip, I refused to open my mouth in the morning because I thought that the branches of the lemon tree that had grown in the night would come out.'

5 'When I was about six or seven years old, I used to believe that a little penguin lived in my refrigerator and his job was to turn the interior light on and off. I used to sit and open the fridge repeatedly, trying to catch him doing it.'

6 'For some reason, I used to think that there was a big red button in the middle of the president's desk, and if he pressed it the whole world would explode. I also thought that it wasn't very well guarded, and I always worried that he would accidentally lean on it.'

7 'One time when I was about to pour a drink from a bottle of diet coke, my sister said "You know, diet coke turns you into a skeleton if you're not fat." I was terrified. Unfortunately for me, her lie worked and I didn't drink any diet drinks until I was in my teens.'

8 'When I was a child, I couldn't understand how a radio made in Japan could play songs in Spanish and English. If they are made in Japan, they should just be able to play Japanese songs.'

9 'During my first few years at school, I kept hearing that "teachers have eyes in the back of their heads" so I thought that when someone became a teacher, they had to have an operation to get an extra set of eyes! I also wondered why a lot of lady teachers had long hair. What's the point of having eyes in the back of your head if you keep covering them up?'

10 'I used to believe (and still do actually!) that animals could watch TV and understand what they were seeing. I had a rabbit that just sat near the screen, staring at it while the show was on, but would look away or do something else when the ads came on. Now my two dogs act in the same way – they sit with me and watch TV, but then start to yawn and stretch during the ads – except dog food commercials, of course!'

Vocabulary
Remembering and forgetting

11 Choose the correct words in the sentences below.

1 Did you remember (*to pay*)/ ***paying*** the phone bill last month?
2 The smell of old buildings always reminds me ***to*** / ***of*** my school days.
3 As soon as she heard his voice, she recognised ***to him*** / ***him*** immediately.
4 The course was so boring that they forgot ***about*** / ***that*** what they'd learnt very quickly.
5 Can you remind me ***phone*** / ***to phone*** Mr Fielding tomorrow morning?
6 Listen to this song. Do you recognise ***it*** / ***about it***?
7 I'll never forget ***meeting*** / ***to meet*** my wife for the first time. It was so romantic.
8 As soon as he saw his boss, he realised he'd forgotten ***to give*** / ***giving*** her the message.
9 Do you remember ***to get*** / ***when we got*** lost in Prague? We realised we'd been walking in a circle for two hours!
10 Can you remind Chris ***about*** / ***to*** the message I left him? I think he's forgotten.

12a Complete the questions with *remember*, *remind*, *forget* or *recognise*.

1 When you argue with a friend, do you __forget__ about it quickly and stay friends?
2 Do you find it easy to __________ people's names?
3 When did you last __________ someone's birthday?
4 Is it easy to __________ your handwriting?
5 Do you __________ people of anyone in your family?
6 How often do you __________ your keys?
7 Can you __________ your first day at school?
8 Do you usually __________ famous people when you see them on TV?
9 Do you __________ meeting your best friend for the first time?
10 What sort of things do people have to __________ you to do?

b 2.3 Listen and check. Then answer the questions about yourself.

Writing
A story

13a Complete the extract from Jenny's letter with *when* and *while*.

... and then on Thursday, I took a new client out to lunch at that French restaurant in the centre of town. What a disaster! Everything was fine at first – we got a nice table, but [1] __when__ they started playing music, we found we were next to the speakers. We changed tables and ordered our meal.
[2] __________ we were waiting for the waiter to bring the wine (he took half an hour), I could see my client wasn't happy. To make it worse, [3] __________ he poured the wine, he spilt it all over my client's suit.
She said, 'Don't worry', but I could see she was very angry, so [4] __________ we were having the first course, the atmosphere was quite tense. Then, [5] __________ we were waiting for the main course, the couple on the next table started having a loud argument!
The worst thing was [6] __________ the bill came, I realised I'd left my credit card at home. I felt really embarrassed and in the end she had to pay. And that wasn't all – I said goodbye to her and went to the car park. But [7] __________ I arrived there, I found that someone had stolen my car [8] __________ we were in the restaurant!

b Use the pictures and prompts to write the story. Use the Past simple and continuous and *when* or *while*. Remember to use *and* and *so* to join parts of a sentence.

Alan is talking about his weekend. On Saturday he went to his friend Kyra's party. Another friend, Guy, offered to take him to the party in his car.

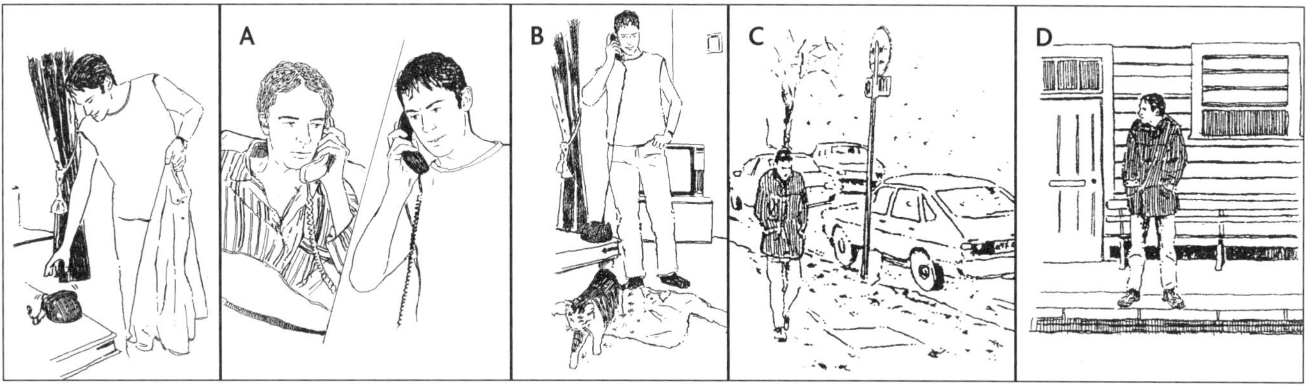

1 **Picture A:** I / get dressed / Guy / phone – say / he / be / ill – I / decide / go by train
I was getting dressed when Guy phoned and said he was ill, so I decided to go by train.

2 **Picture B:** Unfortunately / I / talk to Guy on phone / cat / walk over my shirt – I / have to / iron another one

____

3 **Picture C:** I / walk / station start / snowing – I / get / cold

____

4 **Picture D:** train / delayed because / snowing – it / finally arrive / I / be / frozen

____

5 **Picture E:** I / fall asleep / sit / on the train – miss / station

____

6 **Picture F:** I / get off / next station – decide / walk / Kyra's house. I / reach / end of road / I / realise / I / be / lost

____

7 **Picture G:** I / not have / my mobile – I / look for / phone box / call / taxi

____

8 **Picture H:** I / arrive / Kyra's house / it / be / nearly midnight – people / go / home

____

c 2.4 Listen and compare the story with your version.

03 ACROSS THE GLOBE

Language focus 1
Comparatives and superlatives

1 Find and correct the mistakes in the sentences.

1 Nowadays flying is sometimes ~~more cheap~~ than going by train. *cheaper*

2 The easyest way to book your holiday is on the internet.

3 I'd like to hire a car – I know it's more expensive the train or bus, but it's more convenient.

4 The worse thing about camping is all the insects that you find in your tent!

5 Phuket was our more popular destination last year, so you need to book early.

6 We went to London last August, and it was hoter than I expected.

7 It says in the brochure that New Zealand has the cleanest beaches of the world.

8 Most places are busy during the school holidays than at other times of the year.

9 We always go to the same place – I want to go somewhere more far away this year.

10 I think we should go to Indonesia in March – that's when you get best deals.

2 Some friends are planning to celebrate a birthday at a nightclub. Complete the conversation with the comparative or superlative form of the adjectives in the box.

~~cheap~~	big	central	crowded	expensive	far	friendly
good	quiet	successful				

A: I think All Nite Long looks good: my friends haven't got much money and it's [1] *the cheapest* of the three places. It's also [2] ________ ; they can take 250 people, and it's [3] ________ , so people could get there easily.

B: But Paradiso has got [4] ________ music than All Nite Long – they haven't got real bands there.

C: Actually, I think you should go to Liam's Place: I know it's [5] ________ away than the other two, but because it's small, it's got a [6] ________ atmosphere: the big clubs are too impersonal. Also, it's much [7] ________ if people want to talk.

B: Well, Paradiso isn't noisy at all. I know it's [8] ________ nightclub in town, but for €15 you can get live music and a great atmosphere.

C: But you know it's much [9] ________ than Liam's Place: you often can't get a table.

B: Well, that's because it's [10] ________ club in the north-west at the moment – everyone wants to go there.

A: Hold on! It's *my* birthday, remember, and I want …

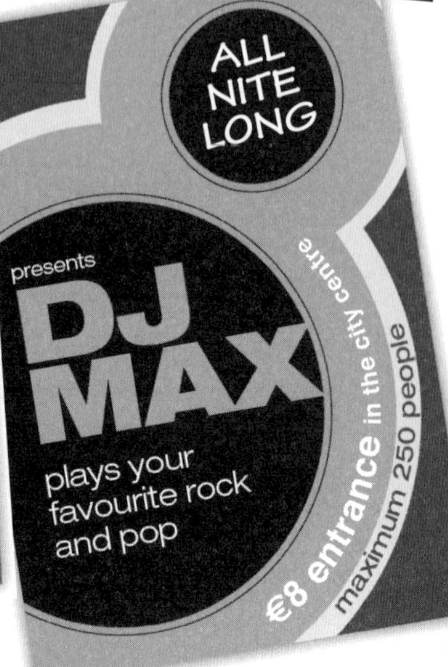

3 Look at the information from a review of digital cameras and choose the correct words in the sentences below.

	F104	Coolshot	Quikpix
size	8cm x 6cm x 2cm	10cm x 7cm x 2cm	12cm x 9cm x 2cm
weight	85g	90g	95g
appearance	9/10	3/10	7/10
reliability	3/10	10/10	9/10
picture quality	5/10	9/10	10/10
easy to use	8/10	10/10	10/10
value for money	2/10	5/10	10/10
popularity rating	★	★★	★★★

1 The Coolshot is ***much heavier / slightly heavier*** than the F104.
2 The Coolshot is ***the second most popular / the most popular*** in the range.
3 The F104 is ***far better looking / slightly better looking*** than the Coolshot.
4 The F104 is ***the most reliable / the least reliable*** of the three.
5 The Quikpix is ***the easiest / one of the easiest*** digital cameras to use.
6 The Coolshot is ***a little bit lighter / a lot lighter*** than the Quikpix.
7 The Quikpix is ***slightly bigger / a lot bigger*** than the F104.
8 The Quikpix has got ***much better / slightly better*** picture quality than the F104.
9 The Coolshot is ***a lot more reliable / a little more reliable*** than the Quikpix.
10 The Quikpix is ***the second best / by far the best*** value for money on the market.

Vocabulary

Features and sights

4 Choose the correct answer to complete the definitions.

1 A place where goods are loaded on and off ships.
docks / a bay
2 A place where Muslims go to pray.
a cathedral / a mosque
3 A building or statue to celebrate people who have died.
a monument / ancient ruins
4 A very, very tall building.
a skyscraper / a village
5 A natural formed curve in the coastline.
a cliff / a bay
6 An area of deep water near the land where ships can stop.
an island / a harbour
7 A man-made river.
a canal / a lake
8 Land that is used to grow plants for food and raise animals.
farmland / rainforest
9 A small mountain.
a hill / a beach
10 A place where products are made in large quantities, often using machines.
a skyscraper / a factory
11 The remains of a very old building or buildings.
ancient ruins / a museum
12 A structure built over a river or road that people can cross over.
a factory / a bridge
13 A special occasion when people celebrate something.
a museum / a festival
14 A grand building where a king or queen lives.
a cathedral / a palace
15 A place where a river falls down over a rock.
a canal / a waterfall

Listen and read

Unusual holidays

5a 3.1 **Listen and read the holiday adverts and answer the questions.**

1 In which holiday do you stay ...

a underground?

The Legendary Ghan Opal Safari

b under the water?

____

c on a boat?

____

d in ice?

____

2 Which two holidays involve diving?

____

3 Which two holidays use a lot of technology?

____

b Listen and read again and answer the questions.

1 How many different types of transport are mentioned in the six holidays?

____

2 Which are only at certain times of the year?

____

3 Why are the houses underground in Coober Pedy?

____

4 What can you see from the plane on the 'Final Frontier' holiday?

____

5 Do you know your route in advance on the 'Storm Chasing' holiday?

____

6 How can you relax on the 'Wilderness Husky Adventures?

____

7 On which holiday can you get married?

____

8 Do you need to be able to dive to go on the 'White Shark Heaven' holiday?

____

The Final Frontier: 3,400 kph

Journey to the edge of space in a Russian Foxbat jetfighter. Arrive in Moscow and spend a day training and preparing for the flight. Then travel at more than twice the speed of sound, to over 24,000 metres above the Earth. Join those few free spirits that have already experienced this journey to the edge of space. At about 32 kilometres above the ground, the curvature of the Earth comes dramatically into view.

In the cockpit of a Russian MiG-25 military fighter plane you're aboard the fastest combat aircraft in the world.

Limited dates.

Contact us direct for details and cost.

Wilderness Husky Adventure

Head up to Lapland and experience the thrill of a husky sledging expedition. Drive your own team of huskies and stay overnight in a traditional wooden lodge, where you can relax and enjoy a traditional sauna. Drive a snowmobile, and with luck see the famous northern lights (aurora borealis), a wonderful natural display of green, red and purple lights in the sky. Finish your trip by staying in the Icehotel – a hotel made completely of ice! This is a really unforgettable and unique short break.

December to April.

Three nights for $2,300.

The Legendary Ghan Opal Safari

This is an extraordinary five-day journey from Adelaide on the south coast to Alice Springs, with an overnight tour to Coober Pedy, where 70 percent of the world's opals are mined. The Ghan is one of Australia's most luxurious trains: you will be travelling across a hostile landscape of desert, salt lakes, mountains and hot springs, but in true comfort whether you travel first class or not.

At Coober Pedy, the temperatures are so extreme (up to 50°C during the day and 0°C at night) that all the houses are built underground as well as the mines. You stay at the Desert Cave Hotel, where the rooms have been cut out of the rock.

Tours are throughout the year and cost $952.

Storm Chasing

Witness spectacular explosive thunderstorms, lightning and tornadoes. Come with us as we follow the storm and get as close as we can, to give you the most exciting experience. Our vans are equipped with the latest storm-chasing technology, like our Weather Radar System, In-Motion Satellite Tracking System, and Lightning Display System that shows storms and lightning up to 500 kilometres away. We travel as far as necessary to see the tornadoes: the chase could take you anywhere in Texas, Oklahoma, Kansas or Eastern Colorado.

May and June only.

Six days for $2,400.

Luxury Under Water

Jules' Undersea Lodge in Key Largo, Florida was originally built as La Chalupa mobile undersea laboratory, the largest and most technically advanced in the world. The Lodge has been completely remodelled to provide guests with luxury living space for up to six people. The interior has two living chambers, with bedrooms and dining and entertainment facilities.

Earn an Aquanaut certificate while enjoying unlimited diving for certified divers, a gourmet dinner prepared by a 'mer-chef', and a gourmet breakfast. If desired, guests may spend several days underwater without surfacing. You can even have your underwater wedding here.

All year round. From $325 per night.

White Shark Heaven, Mexico

The world's ultimate shark dive and fishing adventure is closer than you think. For divers, non-divers and tuna fishermen, discover Isla Guadalupe, one of the world's most exciting new Great White dive sites. Your cage dive and world-class tuna fishing expedition takes you on a five-day live-aboard adventure to the newly discovered and beautiful Isla Guadalupe site off the coast of Mexico. You will have the opportunity to dive by day with Great White Sharks and fish for huge tuna in the hunting grounds of Great Whites and Mako sharks.

Seven-Day Live-Aboard Expeditions:

October to November from $2,380.

Language focus 2

Different ways of comparing

6 Complete the sentences with the words in the box.

~~from~~	as (x2)	completely	different	less
more	similar	slightly	the	to

UK and Australia: the same or different?

1 Australia's climate is different _from_ the UK's.
2 Australian coins look similar ________ British coins.
3 A lot of wild animals in Australia are ________ different from the wild animals that you find in England.
4 Supermarkets in Australia are exactly the same ________ supermarkets in the UK.
5 The cost of living in Sydney is very ________ to the cost of living in London.
6 Houses in the British countryside look very ________ from houses in the Australian countryside.
7 Australian TV programmes are ________ or ________ the same as British TV programmes.
8 Australian road signs are ________ different from road signs in the UK.
9 Daily life in Australia is about ________ same ________ daily life in the UK.

7 Complete the sentences using the words in bold.

1 A meal in the Four Seasons restaurant costs £15. A meal in the Pizza Parlour costs £11.
A meal in the Pizza Parlour costs _less than a meal in the Four Seasons restaurant_. **less**

2 The Manor Hotel is €100 a night. The Park Hotel is €150.
The Manor Hotel isn't ________ **expensive**

3 Savewell supermarket has 2,000 customers a day. Pricerite supermarket has 1,500.
Savewell supermarket ________ **more**

4 There are three trains an hour in the afternoon. There are five trains an hour in the morning.
There are ________ **fewer**

5 The furniture in my sister's flat is more or less the same as Tim's.
The furniture in my sister's flat ________ ________ **similar**

6 The Guggenheim Museum in Bilbao is made mostly of metal. The Guggenheim Museum in New York looks like a concrete multi-storey car park.
The Guggenheim Museum in New York ________ **different**

7 Phil's flat has four rooms and a balcony. My flat's got four rooms and a balcony, too.
My flat's ________ **same**

Pronunciation

Stress and /ə/ sounds in comparative phrases

8a 🎧 **3.2 Listen to the sentences and underline the stress in the phrases in bold.**

/ə/ /ə/ /ə/

1 My city is **a <u>lot</u> bigger than** it was 20 years ago.
2 Peru is **the third largest** country in South America.
3 Australian English is **similar to** British English.
4 The shops here are **not as good as** in my country.
5 There were **fewer** cars here in the past.
6 My language is very **different from** English.

b Listen again and mark the /ə/ sounds. Practise saying the sentences.

Vocabulary

Adjectives for describing places

9 Use the clues to complete the grid.

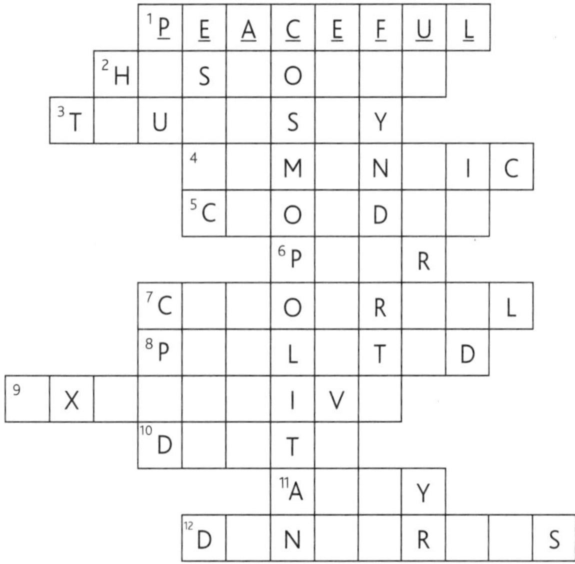

1 quiet and calm
2 important in history
3 popular with tourists
4 makes you think about love or adventure
5 full of people, buildings, etc.
6 people who don't have much money
7 the buildings are painted with bright colours
8 dangerously dirty (to describe air and water)
9 not cheap
10 not clean
11 popular with artists, musicians, etc.
12 not safe

10 Look at the adjectives in the box. Are they positive or negative? Complete the table below.

~~dangerous~~ ~~friendly~~ cosmopolitan modern
colourful spectacular crowded poor
touristy peaceful polluted smart
expensive romantic dirty lively

Positive	Negative
friendly	*dangerous*

Language live

Travel problems

11a Put the words in the correct order to make indirect questions.

1 bus / you / goes / Central Park / Do / to / know / the / when?
Do you know when the bus goes to Central Park?
2 train / Could / arrives / time / the / you / me / what / tell ?
______
3 will / cost / Do / how / know / you / it / much ?
______
4 know / to / Do / change / where / you / have / I ?
______
5 Paris / platform / which / Could / me / goes / the / to / tell / you / train / from ?
______
6 bus / Do / which / know / you / is / this ?
______
7 is / Do / know / you / next / the / when / one ?
______
8 get / you / me / Could / airport / the / tell / to / how / I ?
______

b 🎧 **3.3 Listen and check. Practise saying the questions.**

Writing

Postcards

12a Read the postcard from New York and add the words in the box in the correct place. What types of words are usually left out?

The (x2) there are my is (x2) We're (x2) We'll be We

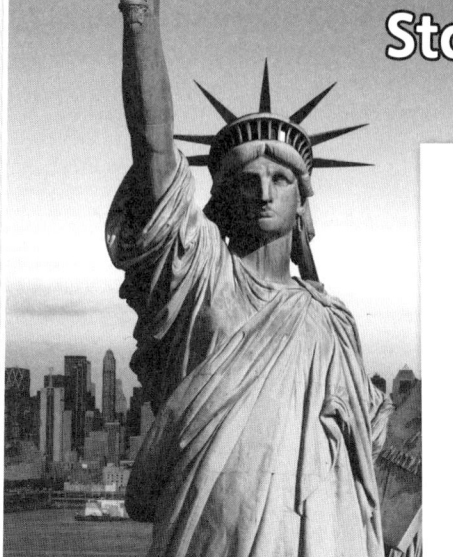

Dear Pete and Sarah,

We're
^ having a great time here in the Big Apple.
Weather brilliant – hot and sunny.
Spent most of today shopping – fantastic department stores here: credit card's not looking too healthy!
Hoping to do some sightseeing tomorrow – Fifth Avenue, Times Square, etc. Nightlife also incredible ... nobody seems to go to bed!
Back in a couple of weeks,

love Sue and Joe
x x x x

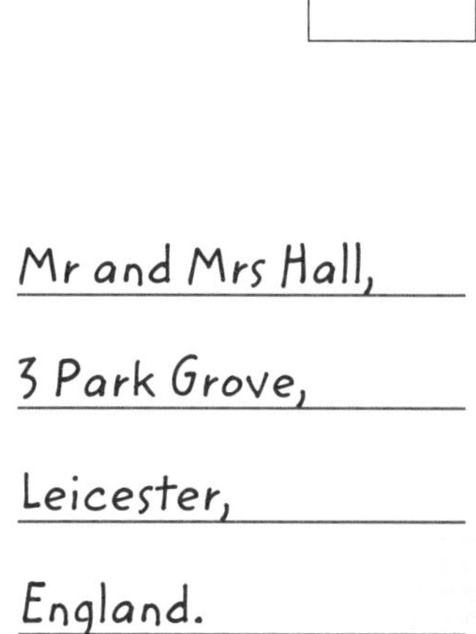

Mr and Mrs Hall,
3 Park Grove,
Leicester,
England.

b Read the postcard from Pisa and circle the words which can be left out.

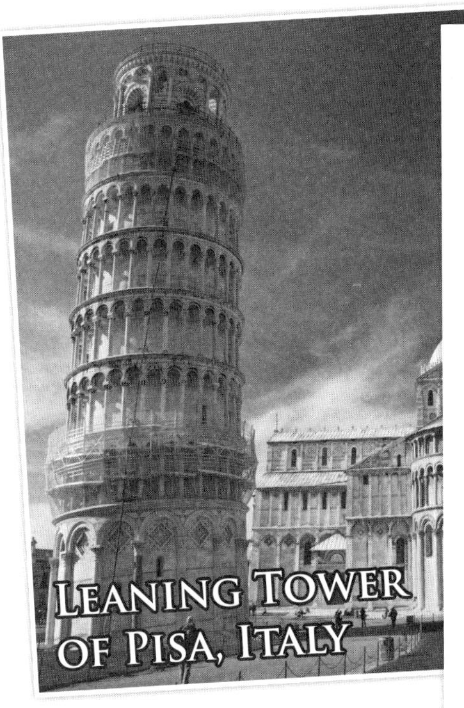

Dear Sam and Julie,

(We) arrived here a couple of days ago – the hotel is small but comfortable, but the food is not great. We're going on a tour of the whole city tomorrow, then we're planning to try some typical pasta dishes for dinner. We hope your family are all well, we'll see you in September.

Love Mark and Tim

Sam and Julie Foster,
School Cottage,
Broadwood,
Gloucester,
England.

04 REAL LIVES

Language focus 1
Present perfect and Past simple

1a Circle the irregular verbs in the 'snake' and write the past participles below. The last letter of one verb is the first letter of the next.

breaknowearereadrinkeeputearingetellendriveateachithrowin

1	*broken*	10	
2	*known*	11	
3		12	
4		13	
5		14	
6		15	
7		16	
8		17	
9		18	

b Complete the conversations with the Present perfect form of the verbs in exercise 1a.

1 **A:** You've got a lot of books. [1] *Have* you *read* them all?
B: No! A lot of them are books I [2]_______ from when I was at school.
A: Oh – I [3]_______ out all my old books from school.

2 **A:** Oh, no! This is the first time I [4]_______ this T-shirt and I [5]_______ it already.
B: Let's have a look. Oh, it's only a small hole; no one will see it.

3 **A:** Mum! Ben [6]_______ his head on the corner of the table! He's crying!
B: Jonathan! How many times [7]_______ I _______ you not to play in here? OK, don't worry, I'm sure he [8]_______ any bones!

4 **A:** Sorry, I can't pick you up from the train station. I [9]_______ the car to Alex.
B: Are you sure that was a good idea? She [10]_______ never _______ an automatic before!

5 **A:** Look – I [11]_______ your photo on our website.
B: That's great! How long [12]_______ you _______ how to build websites?

6 **A:** Who [13]_______ all the biscuits that were in this tin?
B: I don't know, Mum.
A: Hmm, and someone [14]_______ all the cola, too.
B: Maybe it was a burglar!

2 Read the interview with Zoe, a singer in a pop group, and choose the correct words.

Interviewer: Well, it's nearly the end of December and your single [1] ***was*** / ***has been*** number 1 all month. You must be very pleased.

Zoe: Oh yes, of course. [2] ***it was*** / ***it's been*** an incredible year for us – we [3] ***already had*** / ***'ve already had*** two number 1 songs this year and we [4] ***did*** / ***'ve done*** a tour of the UK.

Interviewer: OK, tell us how it all [5] ***started*** / ***has started***.

Zoe: We only [6] ***formed*** / ***have formed*** the group in January, and since then we [7] ***spent*** / ***'ve spent*** almost every day together. At first, we only [8] ***played*** / ***have played*** other people's songs and we [9] ***didn't start*** / ***haven't started*** writing our own songs until we [10] ***found*** / ***'ve found*** our manager, Brian.

Interviewer: Uh huh ... so when [11] ***was*** / ***'s been*** your first big concert?

Zoe: Well, that was two months ago, and around the same time Brian [12] ***got*** / ***'s got*** us a recording contract.

Interviewer: Yes, and your album [13] ***went*** / ***'s gone*** to number 3 in the charts the week it was released. So, what's next?

Zoe: Well, we're working on some new songs and we [14] ***just agreed*** / ***'ve just agreed*** to do a US tour.

Interviewer: Great! Well, we all wish you the best of luck and thank you for coming on the programme.

3 **Find and correct the six mistakes in sentences 1–10 below.**

1 ~~Have you seen~~ *Did you see* the news last night?

2 Carrie's a really close friend – we knew each other for ages.

3 Hello, er ... sorry, I forgot your name.

4 Jeff's never broken a promise before.

5 Oh, that's a nice watch. How long did you have it?

6 My boss was late for work every day last month.

7 Look! It's stopped raining!

8 I see your team's in the final. Did they ever win the cup?

9 We didn't play tennis together since the summer.

10 I can't find my keys – has anyone seen them?

4a **Complete the extract from an article called *Famous Mums and Dads* with the Present perfect simple or Past simple form of the verbs in brackets.**

famous mums and dads

It [1] *was* (be) my birthday yesterday: I'm 14 years old. Some people say I'm lucky but I don't think so. Imagine, in my life I [2]________ (go) to eight different schools and I [3]________ (never stay) anywhere long enough to make a best friend. We [4]________ (live) in so many different houses that I can't remember some of them. In fact, last year we [5]________ (move) house three times. It's true, there are some good things. I [6]________ (meet) some really famous people and we [7]________ (have) some great holidays – I [8]________ (go) to Disneyland at least four times, but never with mum and dad. When I [9]________ (be) young, I always [10]________ (have) a nanny, and she [11]________ (take) me on holiday. I'm staying with my aunt and uncle at the moment because my dad's making a film in France and my mum [12]________ (go) to Los Angeles.

b **4.1 Listen and check.**

5a **Put the words in the correct order to make sentences.**

1 ten / film / ago / The / started / minutes
The film started ten minutes ago.

2 to / Stefano / Did / yesterday / class / come ?
____

3 unit / done / far / I've / the / so / exercises / all / this / in
____

4 brother / the / years / seen / only / her / in / She's / twice / ten / last
____

5 English / 2010 / started / in / learning / I
____

6 2005 / here / He's / since / lived
____

7 young / favourite / was / were / you / your / game / What / was / when ?
____

b **4.2 Listen and check. Practise saying the sentences.**

Pronunciation

Linking in time phrases

6a **4.3 Listen and tick the sentence with the linking you hear.**

1 **a** I've been looking for a flat for about a month. ✓
b I've been looking for a flat for about a month.

2 **a** They've played ten games since August.
b They've played ten games since August.

3 **a** She's only been here for a couple of minutes.
b She's only been here for a couple of minutes.

4 **a** I've been writing this report since eleven o'clock.
b I've been writing this report since eleven o'clock.

5 **a** I've been living in Canada since I was eight.
b I've been living in Canada since I was eight.

6 **a** He went to Brazil a couple of months ago.
b He went to Brazil a couple of months ago.

b **Listen again and check your answers. Practise saying the sentences.**

Listen and read
Johnny Depp

7a 4.4 Listen and read the biography of film star Johnny Depp and put the life events in the correct order.

- **a** He became a teen idol. ☐
- **b** He directed a film. ☐
- **c** had two children ☐
- **d** He had a job selling pens over the phone. ☐
- **e** He met an actor who persuaded him to try acting. ☐
- **f** He played a part in a horror film. ☐
- **g** He played the guitar in a band. 1
- **h** He was voted one of the 'beautiful people'. ☐

Johnny Depp
Born: June 9, 1963
Where: Owensboro, Kentucky

Rare among American actors, Depp has made a name for himself, effortlessly switching between mainstream Hollywood movies and more 'out of the ordinary' projects. Talking about his choice of roles, he once said: 'With any part you play, there is a certain amount of yourself in it. There has to be, otherwise it's not acting. It's lying.' Highlights of a richly diverse career include *Edward Scissorhands*, *Sleepy Hollow* and *Pirates of the Caribbean*.

Depp dropped out of school at 16 to concentrate on a career in music, playing the guitar (he played with more than 20 bands). However, his musical career failed to take off, and he found himself selling pens over the phone to pay the bills. His lucky break came when make-up artist Lori Allison, to whom he was briefly married, introduced him to Nicolas Cage. Although at first they did not like each other, they later became good friends and Cage persuaded him to try acting. Depp signed on with Cage's agent, and made his feature film debut in Wes Craven's horror film *Nightmare on Elm Street*, in which the character he played was eaten by his bed. After that, he had his first screen leading role in *Private Resort*.

Depp went on to achieve teen idol status in the TV series *21 Jump Street*, but after four seasons, he wanted out, with the hope of making the transition to the big screen.

He starred in *Cry-Baby*, followed by Tim Burton's *Edward Scissorhands*, after which he went on to win considerable critical acclaim in *Ed Wood*, a reunion with Burton. Depp made his feature directorial debut with *The Brave* in 1997, a film he also co-wrote and starred in. Premiering at the Cannes Film Festival, the film also featured Marlon Brando, but earned mostly negative reviews, with most critics blaming its weak script. *Sleepy Hollow* teamed him with director Burton yet again, before he starred in Ted Demme's *Blow*, and appeared in the thriller *From Hell*, about Jack the Ripper.

Off screen, his good looks and 'bad boy' image (he was once arrested for attacking intrusive paparazzi with a wooden plank) have earned him a lot of media attention. He was voted one of the 50 most beautiful people in the world by *People* magazine in 1996. He has also had his fair share of celebrity romances. When his engagement to *Edward Scissorhands* co-star Winona Ryder ended, he had a tattoo (one of about 13), which said 'Winona Forever', altered by laser to get rid of the last two letters of her name. His relationship with model Kate Moss also ended abruptly in 1998, when he started dating French singer-actress Vanessa Paradis. They now have two children, Lily-Rose Melody and Jack.

More recent work has included *Pirates of the Caribbean* with Geoffrey Rush, *Once Upon a Time in Mexico, Alice and Wonderland* and *Dark Shadows*.

b Listen and read again and answer the questions.

1 Why is Johnny Depp a 'rare' actor?

____

____

2 What does he describe as 'lying'?

____

____

3 Why did he get a job selling pens over the phone?

____

____

4 Why has Nicholas Cage been important in his career?

____

____

5 What was strange about his first film role?

____

____

6 Who was he popular with in *21 Jump Street*?

____

____

7 What was his involvement in *The Brave*?

____

____

8 Which film director has he made many films with?

____

____

9 Has he still got the tattoo of Winona Ryder's name?

____

____

10 Who was his co-star in *Pirates of the Caribbean*?

____

____

Vocabulary
Life events

8 Complete the phrases in the article with the correct form of the verbs in the box.

~~make~~	move	go	graduate	get (x4)
leave (x2)	pass	bring	fall	change
retire	buy	lose		

From Bottom of the Class to Businesswoman of the Year

At the age of 60, Tessa Daley, director of Newsgroup Publishing, has it all: she has become so successful that she seems to be on TV or in the papers every week, and she has [1] *made* more money than most of us could dream of. But this is the woman who failed all her exams and [2]______ school with no qualifications.

'I hated school and couldn't wait to get away and start work. I [3]______ a job at a local newsagent's. I loved working there because I could read all the magazines, but unfortunately I [4]______ my job two weeks later – for reading magazines and forgetting to serve the customers!'

One of the customers was Simon, a good-looking journalist, who she [5]______ in love with. They [6]______ engaged six weeks after they first met, then got married at the end of that year. Tessa devoted the next 16 years of her life to being a wife and [7]______ up her children. Simon [8]______ jobs a lot during those years, and the family [9]______ house several times. The disruption had a disastrous effect on the marriage and they [10]______ divorced when the oldest child was 15.

'For a long time there was a big gap in my life and I didn't know what to do. My daughter persuaded me to [11]______ home, and [12]______ to university to do media studies.' Tessa worked hard and [13]______ her exams with the best grades in her year. 'The day I [14]______ from university was the proudest day of my life.'

Her life has been on the up and up since then. Since joining Newsgroup publishing she has [15]______ promotion after promotion, gradually working her way to the top. She has just [16]______ a new house and launched a new magazine and is busier than ever: she has no plans to [17]______ yet!

Language focus 2

Present perfect simple and Present perfect continuous

9 **Complete the sentences with the Present perfect continuous form of the verbs in the box.**

~~read~~ cry go phone look not work rain study talk use

1 You *'ve been reading* that book for ages – haven't you finished it yet?
2 My brother ________________ a lot recently about moving to Canada, but I don't know if he will.
3 We ________________ the same recipe for our famous 'Chocolotti' biscuits for the last 50 years, and it's still a secret.
4 Joseph ________________ to evening classes since the summer, but he still can't say 'What's your name?' in Russian!
5 ________________ Kerry ________________? Do you know what's wrong?
6 I ________________ here very long – do you know where the stationery cupboard is?
7 Excuse me, Marcia, a reporter from *Vanity Fair* ________________ all morning – could you speak to her now?
8 How long ________________ it ________________? I haven't got an umbrella with me.
9 We ________________ for a flat for a month now, but we can't find anywhere we both like.
10 Selim ________________ for his exam so much recently, I hope he does well.

10 **Complete the sentences with the words in brackets and *for* or *since*.**

1 Jo's had toothache *for three days.* (three days)
2 Frankie hasn't been to the dentist ________________. (six months)
3 I've been studying history ________________. (a year)
4 Jane's been feeling sick ________________. (last night)
5 Pete's been on a diet ________________. (two weeks)
6 I haven't done any exercise ________________. (months)
7 I've been doing aerobics ________________. (this time last year)
8 She hasn't been feeling well ________________. (her operation)
9 They haven't been to the cinema ________________. (ages)
10 We've been married ________________. (1997)

11 **Choose the correct answers.**

1 I***'ve been knowing*** / ***'ve known*** Susan for about five years.
2 Mum had to take Tim to the dentist because he***'s been breaking*** / ***'s broken*** his tooth.
3 My husband***'s been having*** / ***'s had*** his mobile phone for a week and it's already broken.
4 I hope Karen rings soon because Rick***'s been waiting*** / ***'s waited*** by the phone for hours.
5 We***'ve been going*** / ***'ve gone*** to the new sports centre since June. Why don't you come and try it?
6 Giuseppina's English is getting much better. She***'s been practising*** / ***'s practised*** a lot recently.
7 You look much slimmer. Have you ***been dieting*** / ***dieted***?
8 John's boss ***has been deciding*** / ***has decided*** to have a holiday next month.
9 Goodbye and thanks. We***'ve really been enjoying*** / ***'ve really enjoyed*** this evening.

12 **Use the prompts to make sentences. Use the Present perfect simple or Present perfect continuous and for or since.**

1 I / not see / Jeremy / 2010.
I haven't seen Jeremy since 2010.
2 Katalin / write / novels / she retired.
____
3 Sue and Jenny / know / each other / years.
____
4 Finally! We / wait / for you / two hours!
____
5 The band / play / over 100 gigs / they formed.
____
6 Wolf / work / really hard / he got promoted.
____
7 I / be / a member of the party / 20 years.
____
8 Gina / live / with her parents / a while to save money.
____
9 She / training for the marathon / July.
____
10 I / ski / I was a child.
____

13 Match the words in the boxes with the descriptions of the people 1–12.

~~creative~~ talented obsessive courageous
charming determined

1 Well done, you're really good at thinking of new ideas.
creative

2 I thought it was really brave of you to bring up that issue in the meeting.
____

3 Emma never stops talking about her cats. She thinks about them too much, I think.
____

4 Jamie always gets what he wants – he knows how to make people feel good about themselves.
____

5 As long as we give it 100 percent, nothing can stop us!
____

6 I've never found it difficult to play the guitar, I think I was born able to do it.
____

original ruthless dedicated self-confident
inspiring egotistical

7 Priscilla always seems to be sure that she'll succeed. And she usually does.
____

8 Fabio loves telling people how great he is. It's like he's the only person in the world.
____

9 I really admire how hard Ben works, especially since he doesn't earn much money.
____

10 Have you heard Flyjam's music? I've never heard anything like it before.
____

11 Even though she knew many people would lose their jobs, Fran still decided to cut the budget.
____

12 I loved your speech. It really made me excited about what I could do.
____

Vocabulary

Personal qualities

14 Use the clues to complete the grid.

			1 C	R	E	A	T	I	V	E			
2 C			R		G		O		S				
					3 O			G		N			
			4 D		T			M				D	
5 C				M	I		G						
			6 O		S					V			
			7 R		T		L			S			
					8 I			P		R			G
9 S				–	C			F		D			
10 D			I		A			D					
			11 T		L			T					

1 good at using your imagination to make new things
2 brave, without fear
3 completely new and different from anyone else
4 nothing can stop you
5 you have a special quality that makes people like you
6 thinking or worrying about something all the time.
7 determined and firm when making difficult decisions
8 when you make other people feel excited about doing something
9 sure that you can do things well
10 when you work hard at what you do because you care about it
11 having a natural ability to do something well

05 GO FOR IT!

Vocabulary
Word families

1 **Complete the sentences with a noun, verb or adjective from the pairs of words in the box.**

~~success~~/succeed imaginative/imagination fail/failure profitable/profit distractions/distract productive/produce knowledgeable/knowledge improve/improvement

1 The advertising campaign was a great *success* : sales figures are looking very good.
2 It's a nice idea, but I don't see us being able to ___________ from it. Do you really think it will make us much money?
3 I much prefer working at home. There are fewer ___________ and I find it easier to focus.
4 I'm afraid that if we don't see any ___________ in your work, we're going to have to let you go.
5 Jon's ideas for the website are practical, but they're not very ___________ – I'd like to try a more creative designer.
6 Ask Sophie about that. She's very ___________ in that area.
7 Despite all our hard work, this project has been a complete ___________ .
8 We need to ___________ twice as much as last year if we are going to meet demand.

Pronunciation
Word stress in word families

2a **5.1 Listen to the words below and write the number of syllables next to each word.**

1 suc<u>ceed</u> [2]
2 experience [ ]
3 productive [ ]
4 profitable [ ]
5 distraction [ ]
6 imagination [ ]
7 failure [ ]
8 imagine [ ]
9 experienced [ ]
10 improvement [ ]
11 knowledgeable [ ]
12 know [ ]

b **Listen again and underline the stressed syllables. Practise saying the words.**

Language focus 1
Future forms

3 **Complete the conversations with the correct form of *going to* and a suitable verb where necessary.**

1 **A:** It's my 18th birthday in June.
B: *Are you going to have* a party?
A: I haven't decided yet.

2 **A:** My brother's just heard that he's lost his job.
B: Oh, no! What ________________ ?
A: I think he's planning to travel for a while.

3 **A:** Are you really going to give up chocolate?
B: Yes, ________________ . I bought lots of fresh fruit instead.

4 **A:** Have you got any plans for the weekend?
B: Well, David and I ________________ a film on Sunday night.
A: Oh, which one?

5 **A:** Are you nervous about making a speech at the wedding?
B: Yes, but I ________________ about it anymore.
A: No – thinking about it will only make you more nervous.

6 **A:** Lisa's really in love with Alain, isn't she?
B: ________________ him?
A: I hope so. He'd be the perfect husband for her.

7 **A:** I heard that the council have bought that land behind the cinema to build on.
B: Oh, really? What ________________ there?
A: A new shopping mall, I think.

8 **A:** Are you and Annie going to have a holiday this year?
B: No, ________________ . We haven't got any money.

4 Look at the diaries and use the prompts to complete the conversations.

A

10:30–12:00 English lecture
12:30 Daniella – lunch
2:00 squash
3:00–5:00 tutorial Prof. Wiles

B

Tuesday 8th
9:00 Mrs Phillips
10:00 Mr Long
11:00 S Kennedy
12:00 Ms Barnes
1:00
2:00
3:00 afternoon off
4:00
5:00

C

9:00	
10:00	
11:00	meet Carol Harris – new marketing manager
12:00	
1:00	lunch – Gary Parsons
2:00	visit factory
3:00	
4:00	

Diary A

A: Hi Josh. Can we meet some time today to talk about the English assignment?

B: Well, I'm quite busy. I / go / to a lecture this morning and I / meet / Daniella for lunch.

1 *I'm going to a lecture this morning and I'm meeting Daniella for lunch.*

A: What / you / do in the afternoon?

2 ______________________________

B: Well, I / play / squash until three o'clock, then I've got a tutorial.

3 ______________________________

you / do / anything in the evening? I'm free then.

4 ______________________________

A: OK. That's great. See you this evening, then.

Diary B

A: Hello, Dr Haines' surgery.

B: Yes, hello. Could I see the dentist today? I've got a terrible toothache.

A: Well, he / see / patients all morning.

5 ______________________________

B: Um ... what about the afternoon?

A: No, I'm afraid he / have / the afternoon off. Actually, he could fit you in at one o'clock.

6 ______________________________

B: Oh, thank you very much.

Diary C

A: Yes, Mr Riley?

B: Ah, Celia, what time / I / have / lunch with Gary Parsons?

7 ______________________________

A: One o'clock.

B: Well, could you call him and make it a bit later?

A: That's not really possible.
You / leave / at two to visit the factory in Stanmore.

8 ______________________________

B: Oh yes, of course.

5 Complete the sentences with *will* or *won't* and a verb in the box.

~~be ready~~ be get like need pass send take

1 I need these shoes on Saturday. *Will they be ready* (they) by then?
2 We ______________ to order the flowers at least two weeks before the wedding.
3 ______________ (you) late tonight?
4 I don't think you should buy Mum those gloves, she ______________ them.
5 So, the exam's in June. When ______________ (they) us the results?
6 Don't forget to take a sweater. I expect it ______________ cold later.
7 Stop worrying about the exam – you ______________ easily.
8 Why do you want to leave so early? It ______________ very long to get there.

6 Use the prompts to make sentences.

1 **A:** I'm going to spend the summer in Turkey.
B: Really? Where / you / planning / stay ?
Really? Where are you planning to stay?
2 **A:** What time are your grandparents coming?
B: They / due / arrive / at about six.
____
3 **A:** I hear you've bought a new house.
B: Yes, we / hoping / move / next month.
____
4 **A:** Jeannie looks a bit worried.
B: I know, she / about / take / her driving test.
____
5 **A:** What are you going to do with the money you won in the lottery?
B: Well, I / thinking / buy / a new car.
____
6 **A:** Isn't it a bit late in the day to visit your parents?
B: I / intending / spend / night there.
____

Vocabulary
Work

7 Choose the correct answer to replace the definition in bold.

1 Anna has **passed a lot of examinations** but she doesn't have any practical experience.
a good communication skills
b a lot of qualifications (circled)
c responsibility
2 Scott didn't get the security guard job – they said he wasn't **strong and healthy**.
a physically fit
b secure
c creative
3 The job sounds interesting, but I don't want to **start very early and finish late**.
a travel
b be good with money/numbers
c work long hours
4 I left the company because the work was boring and **they didn't pay much**.
a badly paid
b well-paid
c stressful
5 You're so **good at producing new or interesting ideas** – have you ever thought of going into advertising?
a competitive
b well-organised
c creative
6 My parents want me to be a teacher because it's **a job which I'm not likely to lose**.
a competitive
b a secure job
c challenging
7 I thought I would have **a chance to visit different places** with a job in journalism, but I was wrong.
a a secure job
b opportunities to travel
c special training
8 Wouldn't you like to do something more **difficult in an interesting or enjoyable way** than working in a café?
a badly paid
b stressful
c challenging
9 The problem with my boss is he has no **ability to say what he wants to clearly.**
a communication skills
b qualifications
c responsibility
10 Your job sounds **as if it makes you worry a lot**.
a stressful
b secure
c well-paid

8 Choose the best alternatives.

1 Keira wants the promotion, but she doesn't really want the ***responsibility*** / ***communication skills***.
2 You're very ***well-paid*** / ***good with numbers***. Have you ever thought about becoming an accountant?
3 I'd like to become a fashion designer, but it's very ***creative*** / ***competitive***.
4 Paul runs his business well because he's well-***organised*** / ***secure***.
5 Do you need ***special training*** / ***responsibility*** to become an English teacher?
6 My job's difficult at times, but it's also interesting and ***badly paid*** / ***well-paid***.
7 I used to be a manager, but I didn't like working ***long hours*** / ***responsibility***.
8 He didn't get the job interview because he didn't have the right ***responsibility*** / ***qualifications***.

Language focus 2

Future clauses with *if*, *when*, *unless*, etc.

9 Match a question from A with an answer from B. Then complete the answers with the correct form of a verb from the box.

~~finish~~	be	start	get	send	receive

A

a What time do you think you'll be home? [4]
b Can you phone your sister tonight? [ ]
c When can I expect to get the results? [ ]
d Have you finished that report I asked you to write? [ ]
e Is Paulo coming to the party? [ ]
f What are you going to do after you finish university? [ ]

B

1 He'll try to come if he ________ free.
2 Not yet. I can't do it until Lucia ________ me the statistics I need.
3 OK, I'll call her as soon as I ________ home.
4 I'll be on the six o'clock train unless the meeting *finishes* late.
5 I'm not sure yet, but I'd like to travel a bit before I ________ work.
6 I don't know exactly – we'll post them to you when we ________ them.

10 Complete the sentences, using the words in bold.

1 You'll be in Madrid again. Phone me then.
when
Phone me *when you're in Madrid again.*
2 It's going to get dark soon. Let's stop now.
before
Let's stop ________
3 You probably won't get the job. The only way you will is if you can offer something extra.
unless
You won't ________
4 That film will come out soon. I'd like to see it then.
as soon as
I'd like ________
5 The taxi'll come in a few minutes. I'll wait with you.
until
I'll wait ________
6 You could take the 9 a.m. flight. Then you'll be here by lunchtime.
if
You'll ________
7 Come out of the station. You'll see the bus stop on your right.
when
You'll ________
8 I'll get home later. The first thing I want to do is go to bed.
as soon as
I want ________
9 You may want to go somewhere else. If not, I'll book a table at the Wharf Bistro.
unless
I'll ________

Listen and read

Unusual lifestyles

11a 5.2 Four people are talking about their lifestyles. Listen and read the texts. What are their jobs?

1 Gemma is a/an ___________
2 Raoul is a/an ___________
3 Frank is a/an ___________
4 Megan a/an ___________

Gemma

'I absolutely love music and listen to it all the time, even when I go jogging. Of course I have to look after my voice. I do exercises for three hours every day and I take lots of vitamin C. If I get a sore throat, I go straight to bed and rest. I usually try to get at least eight hours sleep a night anyway. ... As for my job – you really can't be shy in this kind of work, and you have to be very patient because sometimes we practise for hours before we get it right. When we're on tour, we work for several weeks with no breaks and you can get really tired. For relaxation, whenever I get a holiday, I go straight to a sunny beach, but the thing I enjoy the most is the great feeling you get from a live audience.'

Raoul

'Well, my work's really quite stressful. Most people think you spend your day chopping vegetables and stirring soup, but it's not that simple. You have to be really careful with the food and keep everything very clean. The big problem is my boss – he shouts at me all the time – even, for example, if I forget to wash up one plate. I just can't do anything right sometimes.
Actually, I'm hoping to find a new job soon because I don't get much time off. I'd like to have more weekends free, to see friends and to spend more time with my two little boys. You know it's strange spending all day with food – when I go home I just want to eat a sandwich or a bag of chips and I'm terribly critical when I eat in a restaurant.'

Frank

'Well, I first got interested because I loved doing them so much myself – I used to do at least one every day. I suppose I've got the right kind of mind really – I enjoy playing around with puzzles, especially word puzzles. So I sent a couple in to a local newspaper and was really surprised when they asked me for more. I suppose it is a strange way to spend your day – surrounded by dictionaries and books, but it's great that I can organise my own time, so I try to finish by two and then I can take my dog for a walk. It's very satisfying though – I love the feeling after I've thought of the final clue, and it all fits together. It's also really nice when people write to me and thank me. Funny really, because I'm just doing what I like.'

Megan

People sometimes ask me if I forget which country I'm in or what time of day it is, but I guess I've got used to it. Last week I was in London and tomorrow I'm going to Hong Kong.
I'm based in Bahrain, and I have a small apartment there, although I sometimes don't spend more than seven or eight days a month there. The thing I like most about my job is the contact with the people from different cultures. The idea that it's a glamorous job is a bit of a cliché – you spend a lot of your time handing out food and drinks and clearing up people's rubbish. I certainly don't feel very glamorous at two in the morning! Actually, there are a lot of things that we're trained to do that people don't realise – like fight fires, deliver babies, survive in the desert or ocean.

b Listen and read the texts again. Are the statements true (T) or false (F)?

1 Gemma has to keep fit. [T]
2 The most tiring part of Gemma's job is when she's on tour. [ ]
3 Gemma hates performing live. [ ]
4 Raoul's boss is quite easy going. [ ]
5 Raoul works a lot at weekends. [ ]
6 Raoul doesn't spend much time cooking at home. [ ]
7 Frank started writing crossword puzzles for a newspaper. [ ]
8 Frank uses a lot of reference material for his job. [ ]
9 Frank has to work long hours. [ ]
10 Megan spends more time in Bahrain than overseas. [ ]
11 Megan thinks her job is glamorous. [ ]
12 Megan's training was quite varied. [ ]

Writing

A letter of reference

12a When Louisa Barry applied for a job through *Horizons Unlimited*, she asked two people to write her a letter of reference. Look at the two letters, A and B. Which is:

1 an employment reference? ______
2 a character reference? ______

A

20 April 2011

To whom it may concern,

I confirm that Louisa Barry has been [1] *employed* as a personal assistant with this organisation for the last three years, and is [2]________ $35,000 per annum. The job of personal assistant carries the following [3]________: dealing with all correspondence and telephone calls, organising meetings, conferences and business trips, preparing presentations and reports. Louisa has excellent computer [4]________ and a very good telephone manner. Her knowledge of French was a real [5]________ when dealing with our Paris office. She is also extremely reliable and hard working.

I would certainly re-employ Louisa as I consider her to have been a valuable member of the company, who consistently [6]________ good results.

Yours faithfully,

Jason Holmes

Jason Holmes

B

15 April 2011

To whom it may concern,

I [1]________ that I have known Louisa Barry for six years. We first met when she attended a Spanish course that I was teaching, and she has [2]________ become a family friend.

[3]________ a student of Spanish, Louisa excelled: she took every opportunity to practise in the classroom, and learnt quickly from her mistakes. She has an extensive Spanish vocabulary, and her pronunciation is very good. As a friend of the family, Louisa has always been kind and thoughtful: she has helped me patiently with computer problems on [4]________ occasions, and has offered to look after my three children when their nanny was not available. If you require any [5]________ information, please do not [6]________ to contact me.

Yours faithfully,

M. Cortes

b Complete the letters with the words in the box.

~~employed~~	achieved	As	asset	confirm
further	hesitate	numerous		paid
responsibilities	since	skills		

c Write a character reference for someone you know.

Language live

Making a formal telephone call

13a You are phoning Mrs Leeson, at Henderson Insurance. Complete the conversation.

A: Good afternoon, Henderson Insurance, Pam speaking. How can I help?
B: Good afternoon, I'd like [1] *to speak to Mrs Leeson*, please.
A: Just a moment, I'll put you through.

C: Hello, Mrs Leeson's office, Sandy [2]________.
B: Hello, [3]________ Mrs Leeson, please?
C: I'll just see if she's [4]________. Can I ask who's [5]________?
B: Jo Spinelli.
C: One moment, please. Hello, I'm afraid she's not in the office at the moment.
B: OK. Could you ask her [6]________?
C: Certainly. Could I [7]________?
B: Yes, it's 4442 123 451.
C: Right, I'll get her to call you back as soon as she comes in.
B: [8]________.
C: Goodbye.

b 5.3 Listen and check.

06 TRUE STORIES

Language focus 1
Past perfect

1 Complete the sentences with the Past perfect form of the verbs in the box.

~~finish~~ do forget have leave make meet sell travel won

1 He asked why I *hadn't finished* the reports.
2 There was no coffee because Mark ________ to buy any.
3 Glenn knew he ________ a lot of mistakes in his English exam.
4 I phoned about the car for sale but the owner ________ already ________ it.
5 The children were very hungry because they ________ any breakfast.
6 I was certain I ________ the keys on my desk, but they weren't there.
7 Diana was sure she ________ Tony before.
8 The children ________ by plane before so they were very excited.
9 Mrs Dunn was angry because most of the students ________ their homework.
10 United's manager resigned because the team ________ any matches that season.

2 Tick the correct ending.

1 Greg felt terrified because ...
  a he's never flown before. b he'd never flown before. ✓
2 How's Susan?
  a I haven't seen her for ages. b I hadn't seen her for ages.
3 The group Just Girls are breaking up and ...
  a they've only been together for three months.
  b they'd only been together for three months.
4 We were all very tired because ...
  a we've just travelled back from Florida.
  b we'd just travelled back from Florida.
5 I love eating here. It's the best restaurant ...
  a I've ever been to. b I'd ever been to.
6 The whole country was in shock because ...
  a the President has died. b the President had died.
7 It was the first time Juventus ...
  a have lost a match. b had lost a match.
8 What's the matter?
  a You've been depressed all week.
  b You'd been depressed all week.

3 Complete the sentences with the correct form of the verb in brackets. (In each sentence, one verb should be in the Past perfect and the others in the Past simple.)

1 As soon as the film *started* (start) Beth realised she *'d seen* (see) it before.
2 I ________ (be) surprised to find that Mr Cole ________ (leave) the day before.
3 Helen ________ (feel) much better after she ________ (have) a good sleep.
4 The rain ________ (stop) by the time we ________ (get) to the beach.
5 After Sarah ________ (know) Alan for a few weeks he ________ (ask) her out to dinner.
6 When Julia ________ (married) Scott she ________ (not realise) he ________ (be married) before.
7 Geoff ________ (not see) his parents for 15 years so he ________ (feel) rather nervous at the airport.
8 The jazz singer ________ (sing) an old blues song that I ________ (never hear) before.
9 When I ________ (write) the letter I ________ (post) it straightaway.
10 Melissa ________ (be) angry because her brother ________ (eat) all the chocolates.

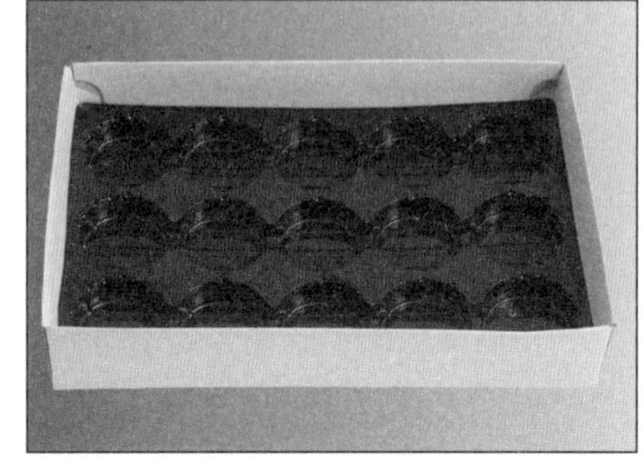

Pronunciation

Past perfect and Past simple in connected speech

4a 🎧 **6.1 Listen and tick the sentences you hear.**

1 **A:** She remembered to call her mum.
  B: She'd remembered to call her mum. ✓
2 **A:** I found the one I was looking for.
  B: I'd found the one I was looking for.
3 **A:** I heard you were in town.
  B: I'd heard you were in town.
4 **A:** John left the book in the car.
  B: John had left the book in the car.
5 **A:** We thought about staying at home.
  B: We'd thought about staying at home.
6 **A:** I booked the table for six o'clock.
  B: I'd booked the table for six o'clock.
7 **A:** He emailed me last week.
  B: He'd emailed me last week.
8 **A:** We met in a restaurant.
  B: We'd met in a restaurant.

b Listen again and practise saying the sentences.

Language focus 2

Reported speech

5a Read the website extract. Then complete the gaps in Stacy's speech.

Stacy, a single woman from London, first met Sam on the internet. Here is some of the information he wrote about himself on the website. Unfortunately, 'Sam Boyd' didn't exist. He was a criminal who already had three 'wives' in different parts of the world. Later Stacy sold her story to a magazine.

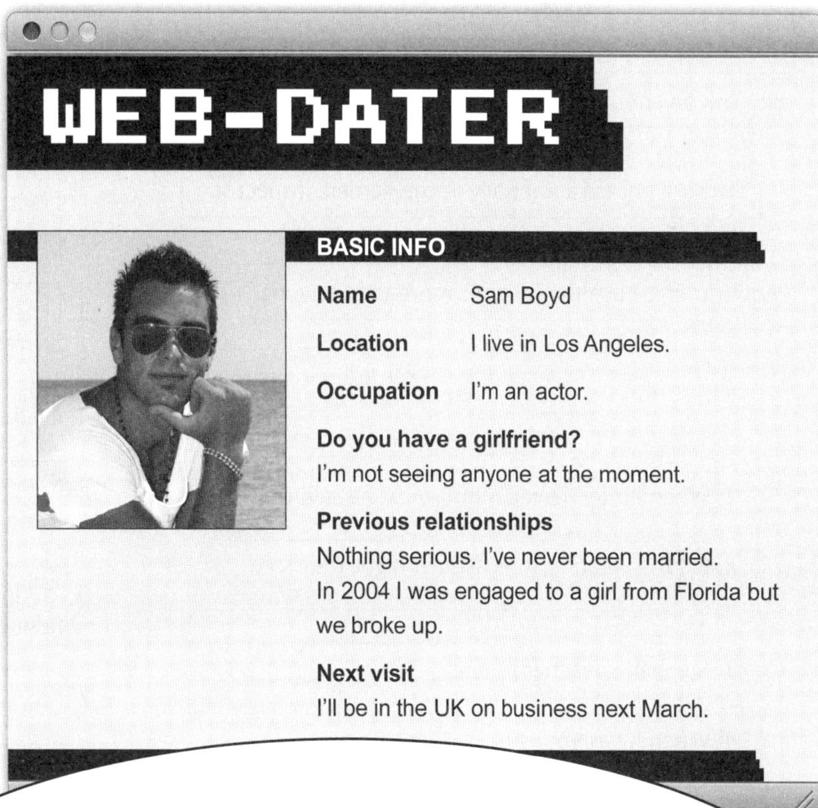

WEB-DATER
BASIC INFO
Name Sam Boyd
Location I live in Los Angeles.
Occupation I'm an actor.
Do you have a girlfriend?
I'm not seeing anyone at the moment.
Previous relationships
Nothing serious. I've never been married.
In 2004 I was engaged to a girl from Florida but we broke up.
Next visit
I'll be in the UK on business next March.

He told me [1] ___*his*___ name [2] ________ Sam Boyd, but I found out later that his real name is Michael Rackham. He said he [3] ________ in Los Angeles and that he [4] ________ an actor but actually he had never had a job or a permanent address. The worst thing was that he said he [5] ________ anyone and that he [6] ________ married, but the police records showed that he already has three 'wives'; one in Texas, one in Turkey and one in Austria. And as for the woman in Florida he said that he [7] ________ engaged to, we found out later that he was talking about his sister who lives there! He told me he [8] ________ in the UK on business in March. He'll get an unwelcome surprise then. The police will be waiting for him!

b 🎧 **6.2 Listen and check.**

6 **Complete sentences 1–10 with a reported form of the statements below.**

Fifty-six people have been killed in a train crash.

I practised eight hours every day.

The world is flat.

I'm working with some great people.

I've just got married.

Stephen's doing very well at maths.

You can be anything you want to be!

I'm sure I heard somebody in the garden, Inspector.

People in Brazil use the internet more than anyone.

It'll rain overnight.

1 When I interviewed Mrs Taylor she said that *she was sure she'd heard somebody in the garden.*
2 On the weather forecast last night they said ______
3 Stephen's teacher told us ______
4 When I was young my father told me ______
5 They said on the news this morning that ______
6 600 years ago, people thought that ______
7 I've just been reading an article in *Computer Monthly* which said that ______
8 My ex-boyfriend sent me a letter saying that ______
9 Wayne Rider, the new tennis star, said that when he was young ______
10 In her email about her new job, Nicky told me that ______

7a **Put the words in the correct order to make reported questions.**

Alessandro has just arrived in London. He wants to improve his English and yesterday he had an interview at a language school. He's telling his friend about the questions he was asked.

1 asked / what / She / my / me / was / name
She asked me what my name was.
2 job / my / wanted / She / was / what / know / to ______
3 I / She / me / in / had / asked / London / when / arrived ______
4 lived / wanted / in / She / if / to / I / Rome / know ______
5 in / was / I / asked / London / She / where / me / living ______
6 'd / long / I / been / me / She / English / learning / how / asked ______
7 I / to / wanted / liked / She / if / know / England ______
8 to / if / She / me / London / 'd / been / before / asked / I ______

b **Write the interviewer's original questions.**

1 *What's your name?*
2 ______
3 ______
4 ______
5 ______
6 ______
7 ______
8 ______

8a Report the questions that Clare was asked.

Clare has just arrived at San Francisco airport where her friend Josh is meeting her. Clare took a long time to go through immigration.

1 Where are you from?
He asked me where I was from.
2 Are you here on holiday?
______
3 Are you travelling alone?
______
4 Did you pack your suitcases yourself?
______
5 Have you been to the USA before?
______
6 How long will you be in the country?
______
7 Do you know anyone in San Francisco?
______
8 Where are you going to stay?
______
9 How much money do you have with you?
______

b 🎧 **6.3 Listen to the questions and report them.**

You hear: *Where are you from?*

You say: *He asked me where I was from.*

Vocabulary

say and *tell*

9a Find and correct the five mistakes in the sentences below.

1 Sorry, what did you ~~tell~~ *say*?
2 The press report said the president had been in an accident.
3 Matthew hasn't told his boss that he's leaving yet.
4 Pat's father said her she should be more polite.
5 Danny told he was going to the USA.
6 Tell to your brother that you're sorry.
7 Mr Stuart said a lot about the new plans.
8 Could you say me your name again, please?

b Choose the correct words, then complete the sentences with the words in the box.

~~joke~~ about difference goodbye no off sorry thank you the truth what

1 Bob ***said / told*** me a good *joke* about an Englishman, an Irishman and a Scotsman.
2 Her teacher ***said / told*** Tanya ______ for being late.
3 If a woman asks you 'Do I look fat in this?' never ***say / tell*** her ______ !
4 Jo left the party without ***saying / telling*** ______ .
5 Look I've ***said / told*** ______ . Can't we just forget about it?
6 Anna's writing a note to her grandparents to ***say / tell*** ______ for her birthday present.
7 Could you ***say / tell*** me ______ your relationship with the president?
8 I asked her if she would go out with me but she ***said / told*** ______ .
9 Can you ***say / tell*** me the ______ between the Canadian and American accent?
10 The girl at the helpdesk was great. I explained the problem and she ***said / told*** me ______ to do.

Listen and read

The world's funniest jokes

10 6.4 The University of Hertfordshire conducted research to find the funniest jokes in the world. 350,000 people visited a special site to submit jokes and to vote for their favourite. Here are some of the results of the year-long experiment. Listen and read jokes 1–5 and match them with pictures A–E.

1 The top joke in the UK

A woman gets on a bus with her baby. The bus driver says, 'That's the ugliest baby I've ever seen!' The woman is furious. She says to a man sitting next to her, 'The driver was extremely rude to me.' The man says, 'Go and speak to him. Go ahead, I'll hold your monkey for you.' ☐

2 The top joke in Northern Ireland

A doctor says to his patient, 'I have bad news and worse news.' 'Oh dear, what's the bad news?' asks the patient. The doctor replies, 'You only have 24 hours to live.' 'That's terrible,' says the patient. 'How can the news possibly be worse?' The doctor replies, 'I've been trying to contact you since yesterday.' ☐

3 The top joke in Canada

When the space organisation NASA first started sending up astronauts, they discovered ballpoint pens would not work in zero gravity. To solve the problem, NASA scientists spent ten years and $12 billion to develop a pen that would write in zero gravity, upside down, under water, on all types of surface, and at temperatures ranging from below freezing to 300°C. The Russians used a pencil. ☐

4 The top joke in Germany

A general noticed one of his soldiers behaving strangely. The soldier used to pick up every piece of paper that he saw, look at it and say, 'That's not it.' This went on for some time until the general arranged for a psychologist to see the man. The psychologist decided that the man was crazy and wrote a letter to say he should leave the army. The soldier picked it up, smiled and said, 'That's it!' ☐

5 The top joke in the world

Two New Jersey hunters are out in the woods when one of them falls down. He doesn't seem to be breathing and he looks very white. The other man takes out his phone and calls the emergency services. 'My friend is dead! What can I do?' The operator says, 'Calm down. I can help. First go and make sure he is dead.' There is a silence, then a shot is heard. Back on the phone, the man says, 'OK, what next?' ☐

Vocabulary
Adverbs for telling stories

11 Complete the sentences from an email about moving to Russia with the adverbs in the box.

~~immediately~~	eventually
fortunately	gradually
obviously	suddenly
surprisingly	unfortunately

As soon as I got to St Petersburg, I [1]*immediately* fell in the love with the city.
I had some problems getting around at first, but [2]____________ the people are very kind and helped me when I got lost on the Metro.
I've started Russian lessons and my speaking is [3]____________ improving.
The weather's been brilliant. [4]____________, there had been no snow until November this year (usually it starts in October).
Last Tuesday it [5]____________ started snowing in the middle of the afternoon at work and it hasn't stopped since then.
My apartment is small but clean and not too expensive. [6]____________ it's a long way from the office and I missed the last Metro home last night.
I was waiting for a taxi when a man came up to me and started talking to me very loudly. He seemed very strange and [7]____________ I felt quite frightened.
A young man came and helped me. He waited with me until [8]____________ a taxi arrived.

Writing
Checking for mistakes

12 Here is a Japanese legend written by a student. The teacher has marked the mistakes using the code in the story. Look at the code and correct the mistakes below.

^ for a missing word
sp for spelling
wo for word order
vf for verb form
ww for a wrong word

The crane

Once there was ^ *a* poor hunter who lived in Japan. One day he was hunting and ^
he find a crane caught in a tree. He felt sorry for the crane and he freed it. vf
Than he went home and forgot about it. ww

A few days later, a lovely woman came to the hunter's house. They felt in love ww
and they got married. His wife new was kind and beautiful but he didn't have wo
enugh money for two people. She saw his problems and offered to weave some sp
fabric so that he could sell it – but she said him that he must never watch her. ww

She stayed in the weaving hut during three days. At last she came out with a ww
beuatiful fabric called Tsuru-no-senba-ori (thousand feathers of a crane). The sp
hunter sold the fabric for a lot gold. The hunter spent all the gold and he ^
asked her several times to make fabric more. The hunter became richer wo
and richer but his wife gradually became thiner and thiner. sp (x2)

Eventually, she said that she can not work because she was too tired. vf
But her husband was greedy and asked her to weave the fabric once longer. ww
Three days passed, then four, then five, but she not did come out of the hut. wo
In the end, on the sixth morning, hunter was so worried that he finally looked ^
through the window of the hut. To his surprising, it was not a woman but a ww
crane that was weaving. Finally, his wife came out with the fabric in arms. ^
She said, 'You have seen my true appearance, so I not can stay with wo
you any longer.' Then she changed into a crane and fly away. vf

07 MUST-SEE!

Vocabulary
Entertainment and television

1 Complete the definitions with the words in the box.

~~advert~~	soap opera	cookery programme
documentary	phone-in	weather forecast
travel news	sitcom	talent show
murder mystery	game show	reality show

1. A short video used to tell people about a product or a service. *advert*
2. Part of a programme which gives you information on whether it will rain, be sunny, etc. tomorrow. ________
3. A show which keeps you guessing about what happened until the last scene. ________
4. A programme which contains factual information about something. ________
5. Part of a programme which gives you up-to-date information on the traffic conditions. ________
6. A show where people compete for prizes. ________
7. A show where people compete by singing, dancing, etc. ________
8. A programme where members of the public can give opinions or ask for advice. ________
9. A programme about ordinary people in unusual or challenging situations. ________
10. A series of amusing stories about the same set of characters. ________
11. A continuing story about the daily lives of a group of characters. ________
12. A programme where you can learn new recipes. ________

Language focus 1
-ing / *-ed* adjectives

2a Complete the letters to a TV magazine with the adjectives in the box.

~~amazing~~	shocking	confused	shocked
pleased	disappointing	annoyed	
disappointed	inspiring		

A

Well done Channel 10 for the brilliant series *City Mysteries*. The acting was [1] *amazing* and the stories didn't try too hard – genuinely interesting without trying to be too [2] ________ . I was so [3] ________ when it finished. Are there plans for a new series?

B

I'm rather [4] ________ about ABC's policy on not showing violence before 9 p.m. I watched *The Precinct* at 8:30 p.m. last Thursday and was [5] ________ at the amount of violence shown. I must say I'm quite [6] ________ with ABC for making my 10-year-old daughter sit through this.

C

I was really [7] ________ when I saw that *Celebrity Spot* was back on SBS. I always look forward to the programme because it has such [8] ________ guests. However, last Friday's show was very [9] ________ – the interviewer asked such stupid questions and hardly gave Rihanna a chance to speak!

b 7.1 Listen and check.

3 Complete the sentences with the correct form of the adjectives in the box.

amazing / ~~amazed~~	annoying / annoyed
inspiring / inspired	shocking / shocked
frustrating / frustrated	irritating / irritated
confusing / confused	embarrassing / embarrassed

1 I was *amazed* by the amount of progress Maria has made with her English since the last time I saw her.
2 It was so ________ . Kim's brother came up to talk to me at the party and I didn't recognise him!
3 Elena got very ________ with Geri for being late for another meeting.
4 Whenever I see a great work of art, I feel truly ________ to create something myself.
5 I wish you'd stop asking me silly questions, it's so ________ !
6 I'm no good at algebra. I just find all those formulas so ________ .
7 I was truly ________ when Oscar made that comment. How could he be so insensitive?
8 I've had a very ________ shopping trip: I couldn't find anything I liked.

Language focus 2

The passive

4 Complete the news stories with the correct form of *be* or *have*.

1 A house in Brazil which *is* made of plastic bottles has won a prize.
2 Pizza-scented bathroom products ______ been created by an Italian cosmetics manufacturer.
3 Stars of the extreme sport 'free running' will ______ shown on TV jumping between buildings and across rooftops.
4 A dog ______ been offered a gold credit card with a $10,000 limit.
5 A mother and daughter, who hadn't seen each other for 17 years, met when they ______ put in the same prison cell in Brazil.
6 A Mexican man who ______ shot in the back and neck says his dog did it.
7 French bus drivers, who ______ banned from wearing sunglasses in summer, are going on strike.
8 An eight-foot-long lizard who has a nerve disorder ______ being treated with acupuncture.
9 Five tourists were rescued by helicopter after they ______ been chased round a field by a bull.
10 A man's neighbours say they ______ being kept awake at night by his dog snoring.

5 Look at the sentences and write questions using the passive form.

1 George was taken to hospital because he had a heart attack. (ask why)
Why was George taken to hospital?
2 The car was stolen between 10 p.m. and midnight. (ask when)
____
3 Tickets for the concert are sold at all large music stores. (ask where)
____
4 The new hospital will be built next to the old one. (ask where)
____
5 The article was written by Urma Mackintyre. (ask who by)
____
6 The open air concert has been cancelled. (ask why)
____
7 Portuguese is spoken in Portugal and Brazil. (ask where)
____
8 Napoleon was known as Boney. (ask what)
____
9 The film was directed by Zeffirelli. (ask who by)
____
10 Forty people have been injured. (ask how many)
____

6 Complete the sentences with the passive form of the verbs in brackets.

1 In the UK, psychology *is taught* (teach) in universities but not usually in schools.
2 The body of a young man ________ (find) in the river yesterday.
3 Thirty-five cars ________ (steal) from the city centre since January.
4 Where ________ the next Olympics ________ (hold)?
5 Knives ________ (not sell) to children under the age of 16.
6 ________ the bridge ________ (build) a long time ago?
7 I'm sorry, but dinner ________ (not include) in the price of an overnight stay.
8 ________ the vegetables ________ (freeze) immediately after you pick them?

7 Read texts A–C and complete the gaps with the best form (active or passive) of the verbs in the boxes above each text.

A

~~cost~~ wear make export

'... and this is the last stage of the production process. As you know, Swift trainers are very expensive, and the reason they [1] *cost* so much is that they [2] ________ of the highest quality leather. We [3] ________ over 10 million trainers to countries all round the world and our shoes [4] ________ by all types of people, from top athletes to children at school.'

B

write give stay be

'... and that [5] ________ a track from the latest album by Didi Brown. The songs on the album [6] ________ by Didi herself when she [7] ________ in Ireland last year. The album is available on download from next week and half the money from the sales [8] ________ to the 'Children In Need' fund.'

C

come open check redesign

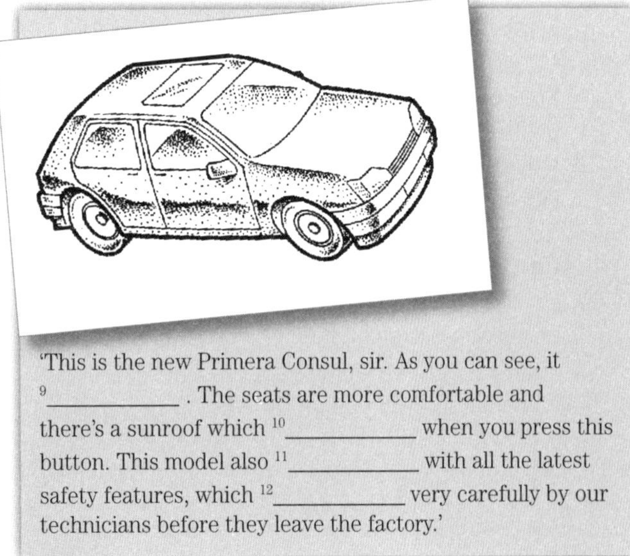

'This is the new Primera Consul, sir. As you can see, it [9] ________ . The seats are more comfortable and there's a sunroof which [10] ________ when you press this button. This model also [11] ________ with all the latest safety features, which [12] ________ very carefully by our technicians before they leave the factory.'

Vocabulary

Extreme adjectives

8a Complete the conversations with extreme adjectives.

1 **A:** I bet Tessa was happy about her exam results.
B: Oh yes, she was absolutely *delighted* .

2 **A:** I'm not going in – the water's ________ !
B: Oh come on, it's not that cold.

3 **A:** You're not frightened of spiders, are you?
B: Oh yes I am – absolutely ________ , in fact.

4 **A:** Have you seen the ________ outfit that Roberta's wearing?
B: Oh yes, she does look a bit silly, doesn't she?

5 **A:** I thought there were some really ________ moments in that film.
B: Did you? I didn't think it was that funny.

6 **A:** And now to the sad news about Ernie Hope.
B: Yes, his death will be a ________ loss for the entertainment industry.

7 **A:** I was ________ when Will told me about his divorce.
B: I know, it was a surprise, wasn't it?

8 **A:** You look hot – do you want a cold drink?
B: Yes, please, it's absolutely ________ outside.

b 7.2 Listen and check.

Pronunciation

Word stress

9a Look at the pairs of words below. Do they have the same (S) or different (D) stress patterns?

1 terrified, excellent [S]
2 astonished, awful [ ]
3 boiling, furious [ ]
4 exhausted, delighted [ ]
5 excellent, hilarious [ ]
6 awful, freezing [ ]
7 hilarious, ridiculous [ ]
8 terrible, furious [ ]

b 7.3 Listen and check. Practise saying the adjectives with the correct stress patterns.

Vocabulary

Entertainment and television

10a Complete quotes 1–13 with the words in the box. You may need to use some of the words more than once.

~~a film~~	a classical concert
a TV drama	a comedy show
a ballet	an opera
a pop video	a play
a musical	a rock concert

1 'The **camera work** was very different. You could see everything from unusual angles.' *a film*

2 'The **jokes** were really funny. I laughed so hard I thought I was going to cry.' ______

3 'The **orchestra** will be performing Pachelbel's Canon in D major.' ______

4 'That was the worst performance of Don Giovanni I've ever seen. The **singing** was truly awful.' ______

5 'The **scenery** was so badly made that parts of it fell onto the stage while the actors were performing!' ______

6 'Although many of the **cast** are unknown, you'll soon start to love them after only a few episodes' ______

7 'Did you see Tiny G.'s new song on The Chart Show yesterday? I know you don't like his music, but the **special effects** are amazing.' ______

8 'Channel 9's new series 'Sorted' is terrible. The **plot** could have been written by a five-year old.' ______

9 'Watching the 'making of' documentary, you could see that the actors are as funny off **the set** as they are on it.' ______

10 'Although the **acting** was terrible, the songs were catchy and the performers looked glamorous.' ______

11 'If you go to see Swan Lake, be prepared to see some truly fantastic **dancing**.' ______

12 'The **costumes** in the new production of 'Ghost' at the Royal Theatre are designed by Marc Lombard.' ______

13 'I don't really like their songs in general, but the way the band shouted the **lyrics** made you pay attention!' ______

b Replace the words in bold below with a word in bold from exercise 10a.

1 The **clothes** were very realistic and had amazing detail. *costumes*

2 I couldn't hear the **words** in the song as she doesn't sing very clearly. ______

3 I don't like films with a complicated **story**. ______

4 The play has a talented **group of actors**. ______

5 We won a competition to visit the **place where the TV show is filmed**. ______

6 What did you think of the **unusual images and sounds** in the film? ______

7 I thought the **painted background** in the play was very realistic. ______

8 Lucia plays violin with an amateur **group of classical musicians** at the weekend. ______

Listen and read

Customer reviews

11a 7.4 Listen and read customer reviews 1–3. Which is a review of:

1 a film? _______
2 a book? ________
3 a CD? _______

1
Reviewer:
Greg from London

More of the King's top tunes and a follow-up to last year's smash hit album *Elvis Number Ones*, released at a time when the King's popularity is at an all time high. Two tracks stand out from the norm: a curious remix of *Rubberneckin'*, and an unreleased version of *I'm a Routabout*. Both songs are enjoyable to listen to, but not strong enough to be hits.

The rest of the album sounds like many an Elvis compilation of the last two and a half decades, with plenty of old classics and fans' favourites. Some of the highlights which non-fans as well as fans may enjoy are: *Loving You, I Need Your Love Tonight, Bossa Nova Baby* (potential remix material here?), *Always On My Mind* and *Moody Blue*. *Moody Blue* is a very good song, although recorded at a time when Elvis was not in great health. I believe this could have been a big smash hit for Elvis if it had come along in 1970–73 when he may have had more energy to put into the song, rather than 1976–77.

If you don't already have a lot of the songs on this CD then this is for you, especially as the technical sound quality of the songs will be better than on previous releases.

2
Reviewer:
Frankie from Wales

This movie is far too short when you compare it to its predecessors, but in its 109 minutes you get more action than the first two movies combined, and you also get a great story.

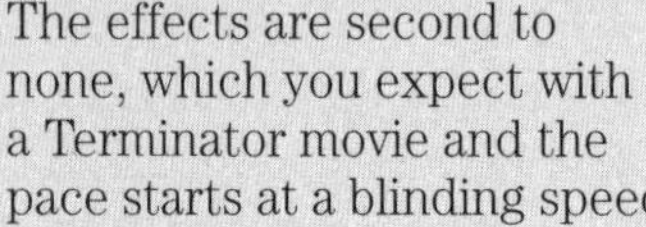

The effects are second to none, which you expect with a Terminator movie and the pace starts at a blinding speed and never slows. There are some great moments of continuity from the first two movies and one or two cameos and returns of past characters. The movie is also not afraid to have its funny moments, such as Arnie walking into a nightclub naked on ladies' night in search of clothing. The scene also gives some light relief from the movie's otherwise somewhat negative feel as humanity rolls closer to impending disaster.

While I may sound a little unpopular, I rate this instalment higher than its predecessors: the director does a better job than Cameron could ever hope to do. This is a fantastic chase movie, even more so than T2 ever was, and with T4 already written, I am eager to see what will happen next in the saga.

And no, I didn't miss Linda Hamilton as much as I thought I would: this movie has proved that it can do just as well, if not better without her presence.

3
Reviewer:
Jed Barker from the USA

Until this summer, I have been guilty of writing off the Harry Potter books as 'mere children's books'. But after finally taking the time to read them, I realised what I have been missing all this time. Sure, they are kid-friendly, but they are witty, clever and can be enjoyed by even a college student like myself. And I am very pleased to say that they get better and better with each instalment.

Order of the Phoenix takes a distinctly dark tone that was hinted at in *Goblet of Fire*. Harry is not a young kid any more, and yes, he is angry a lot, but with everything that he has had to deal with, he has every right to be. There is, of course, Voldemort on the loose and the Ministry of Magic trying to cover it up (a source of political satire in this novel). There is also a much-hyped 'death of a central character'. I won't reveal who the unfortunate person is, but I was quite upset when Rowling killed him/her off. That is yet another testament to her genius, the fact that she makes you care so much about her characters.

I thoroughly enjoyed this book. Anyone with a sense of fun and imagination should. It may not be a literary masterpiece, but it doesn't need to be. It's just fun. And yes, it's long, but it moves so fast that you can hardly believe that there are nearly 800 pages!

b Listen and read again. Are these statements true (T) or false (F)?

The reviewer of the Elvis Presley CD thinks that:

1 Presley's music is very popular at the moment. T
2 *Bossa Nova Baby* has been remixed. ☐
3 *Moody Blue* was a smash hit. ☐

The reviewer of *Terminator 3* thinks that:

4 it has more action than the previous two movies, although it is shorter. ☐
5 the funny scene in the nightclub was a good idea. ☐
6 Linda Hamilton should have been in the movie. ☐

The reviewer of the Harry Potter book:

7 used to think that Harry Potter books were only for children. ☐
8 doesn't understand why Harry Potter is angry a lot. ☐
9 admires Rowling's ability to create sympathetic characters. ☐
10 thinks that the book is too long. ☐

Language live

Making a social arrangement

12a Choose the correct answers to complete the conversations.

1 A: ***I'm phoning to ask*** / ***I'll phone to ask*** if you'd like to come over for dinner.
B: That sounds great. What time shall I come?

2 A: I've got two tickets for *Rejection* at the cinema on Saturday. ***Would you like to come?*** / ***Do you like to come?***
B: ***I sorry*** / ***I'm sorry***, I can't. It's my sister's birthday.

3 A: Great, can you give me a ring ***when you get there?*** / ***when you'll get there?***
B: OK, will do.

4 A: Are you free later? Do you want to go for some food?
B: Yeah, ***I'd love to!*** / ***I'd love!***

5 A: ***What about meet*** / ***What about meeting*** at Phil's flat first?
B: OK, ***I'll see you there.*** / ***I'm seeing you there.***

6 A: ***Are you free*** / ***Do you free*** this evening?
B: No, sorry ... ***I'm having*** / ***I'll have*** dinner with Cheryl.

b 7.5 Listen and check.

Writing

Email invitations

13a Read emails A–F and match the three invitations with their replies.

1 an invitation to a meeting ___; reply ___
2 a wedding invitation ___; reply ___
3 an invitation to stay for the weekend ___; reply ___

A We're having a few people to stay for the weekend from 17-19 August and I was wondering if you'd like to come. We're hoping it'll be nice enough to have picnics, go swimming, etc. Let me know as soon as you can, hope you're well, regards

B That's great news. Of course I'd love to come to the wedding. You'll have to send me the wedding list. Or I should just buy you a surprise present?!

C Hello there. I hope you're not too busy. Could you possibly come to a meeting tomorrow at 10:30, to discuss the new book? I'm sorry it's such short notice.

D Thanks very much for the invitation. I'm afraid I've arranged to go to my parents' wedding anniversary party that weekend, so I won't be able to come. What a shame - some other time, perhaps?

E Yes, I think I can make it. I'll have to leave before 12:00 though, because I've got to be on the other side of town for lunch. I hope that's all right and look forward to seeing you tomorrow.

F I know it's a strange time to be sending email, but I can't sleep! Jon and I have decided to get married and I wanted you to be the first person I invited to the wedding. It's going to be in Dublin on Saturday September 9th. I'll send you a proper invitation in the post - but I do hope you can come. If you're still awake, please reply!

b Look at the emails again and underline useful phrases for inviting, and for accepting or refusing an invitation.

c Write an invitation and show it to your teacher.

08 SOCIAL LIFE

Language focus 1
Polite requests

1 In conversations 1–7, is B saying 'yes, it's OK,' or 'no, it's not OK' to A's request? Choose the best answer, Yes or No.

1 **A:** Can I pay by visa?
B: I'm afraid we only accept cash.
Yes / *No* (circled)

2 **A:** Is it OK if I bring Susanna to the party?
B: Sure, no problem. It'll be nice to see her.
Yes / *No*

3 **A:** Do you mind if I phone you back later?
B: I'll be out until three. Try after that.
Yes / *No*

4 **A:** Could you possibly have a look at my computer?
B: Of course.
Yes / *No*

5 **A:** I'm going to be late home. Would you mind feeding the cat for me?
B: Of course not.
Yes / *No*

6 **A:** Do you mind waiting for a few minutes? The doctor's busy at the moment.
B: Sorry, but I have to catch a train.
Yes / *No*

7 **A:** Do you think you could come back later?
B: Certainly.
Yes / *No*

2 Put the words in the correct order to make polite requests.

1 me / you / Can / a / lend / pencil ?
Can you lend me a pencil?

2 here / I / mind / if / you / sit / Do ?
____

3 speak / please / more / you / Could / slowly ?
____

4 bag / minute / you / after / mind / a / Would / for / looking / my ?
____

5 possibly / $20 / borrow / I / Could ?
____

6 mind / your / down / turning / Would / you / music ?
____

3a Find and correct the mistakes in the polite requests.

1 **A:** Is *it* ^ all right if I close the window?
B: Yes, go ahead.

2 **A:** Would you helping me with my suitcase?
B: I'm sorry but I've got a bad back.

3 **A:** Could I pass the salt, please?
B: Yes, here you are.

4 **A:** Would you to bring us the bill, please?
B: Certainly, sir.

5 **A:** Do you mind I go now?
B: No, that's fine. I think we've finished.

6 **A:** Do you mind getting me some milk?
B: Of course not. How much do you need?

7 **A:** Could I possible have a look at your newspaper?
B: Of course.

8 **A:** Would you mind to answer my phone while I'm out?
B: I'm afraid I can't. I'm just going to a meeting.

b 8.1 Listen and check. Then listen and repeat the conversations, using polite intonation.

4 Look at situations 1–9 and complete each question to make it polite.

1 You want to pay by credit card.
Can *I pay by credit card?*

2 You want to borrow your friend's camera.
Do you think ______

3 You didn't hear what your classmate said. You want her to say it again.
Could ______

4 You've written a letter in English. You want your teacher to check it.
Would you mind ______

5 You can't hear what your flatmate is saying because of the radio. You want him to turn it down.
Would ______

6 You need ten euros. You want your colleague to lend it to you.
Do you think ______

7 You haven't finished your essay. You want to give it to your teacher a day late.
Do you mind if ______

8 You need to use your colleague's computer.
Could I possibly ______

9 Your friend asks you to go to the cinema with her. You can't tell her until tomorrow.
Is it OK ______

Pronunciation

Polite intonation in requests

5a 8.2 **Listen to the requests below. You will hear them twice. Which one sounds more polite, A or B?**

1 Do you mind if I sit here? [A]
2 Can we have the bill, please? [ ]
3 Could you open the window, please? [ ]
4 Is it all right to turn on the radio? [ ]
5 Excuse me, can you pass me my coat, please? [ ]
6 Would you mind lending me €5 until tomorrow? [ ]

b **Listen to the polite requests again. Practise saying each one using polite intonation.**

Language focus 2

will and *shall* for instant responses

6a **Write full answers using *I'll* or *Shall I …* for offering. Add any necessary extra words.**

1 **A:** I forgot to tell Jack about the meeting.
B: I / phone / him / you?
Shall I phone him for you ?

2 **A:** I'm really thirsty.
B: I / get / you / drink.
______

3 **A:** Hello, IT Support? My printer isn't working.
B: OK / I / come over / have / look.
______

4 **A:** I think I'm going to miss my train.
B: Don't worry / I / take you / station
______

5 **A:** This CD is great!
B: I / lend / it / you / you want.
______

6 **A:** That old lady's having trouble with her bags.
B: I / go over / help?
______

7 **A:** Can you give me some information about holidays in Greece?
B: Certainly. I / get you / brochure.
______

8 **A:** Sandra loves these sandals.
B: I / buy / a pair / her birthday?
______

b 8.3 **Listen and check. Then listen and repeat the offers.**

7 **Choose a sentence from each box, to make conversations for A and B, in situations 1–7.**

A

~~The black ones look really nice, Madam. Are they comfortable?~~
There's a problem with the time of my flight, I'm afraid.
Is there anything good on TV tonight?
Hi! Nice to see you. Come in and have a coffee.
Are you ready to order?
Has Mrs Williams in the Accounts Department returned from lunch yet?
I've got a problem with my shower. It isn't working.

B

OK, but I've got a meeting later so I'll need to leave by 11.
Yes, I'll have the fish.
OK, shall I see if I can change it for you?
Yes, very – I'll take them.
I don't know – shall I have a look in the newspaper?
Yes, she has. Shall I put you through?
I'll send someone up straightaway. Which room is it?

1 In a shoe shop
A: *The black ones look really nice, Madam. Are they comfortable?*
B: ____________________

2 In a hotel
A: ____________________
B: ____________________

3 In a travel agent's
A: ____________________
B: ____________________

4 Visiting a friend's house
A: ____________________
B: ____________________

5 In a restaurant
A: ____________________
B: ____________________

6 Phoning someone's office
A: ____________________
B: ____________________

7 At home in the evening, relaxing
A: ____________________
B: ____________________

8 **Complete the conversations with the correct form of *will* or *going to* and verbs in the box.**

~~go~~ go see buy spend do visit give walk throw

1 A: It's Paul's birthday today.
B: Is it? I *'ll go* and get him a card.

2 A: Do you want to take a taxi home?
B: No, I think I ________ . It's not far.

3 A: Would you like to go out for a meal tonight?
B: Thanks, but I can't. Sue and I ________ the evening with my parents.

4 A: I've just seen Mark go into the café next door.
B: Really? I haven't seen him for ages. I ________ in and say hello.

5 A: What are you doing this weekend?
B: I ________ my brother and his girlfriend. They're having a barbecue.

6 A: What are you doing this weekend?
B: I'm not sure. Maybe I ________ a film.

7 A: We don't have any more bread.
B: OK, I ________ some when I go to the shop.

8 A: Are you running every day?
B: Yes, I ________ a marathon next month.

9 A: That old pullover looks terrible. It's so old.
B: Yes, you're right. I ________ it away.

10 A: I've got an old bike I don't use any more. Do you want it?
B OK. I ________ you £100 for it.

Vocabulary
Social behaviour

9 Complete the sentences with the correct form of a word/phrase from box A and a word/phrase from box B.

A

~~kiss~~ hug go out shake take refuse
share insist invite pick

B

~~on both cheeks~~ up bill party home
hands drive date pay each other

1 In my country, when two women meet they usually *kiss* each other *on both cheeks*.
2 The show starts at seven so I'll __________ you __________ at six.
3 The food took an hour to arrive, and tasted awful, so we __________ to __________ the bill.
4 Have you heard? Apparently Owen and Liz __________ on a __________ last night!
5 Ali and Sophie were so excited when they heard the news that they __________ __________ and cried with happiness.
6 Jamie was so nice when we went out. He even __________ me __________ at the end of the evening.
7 Has Jenny __________ you to her __________ on Saturday? We could go together.
8 Do people usually __________ __________ when they do business in your country?
9 I said I'd get the bus, but he __________ on __________ me to the party.
10 Is it common for men and women to __________ the __________ when they go out for dinner in your country?

10 Correct the wrong word in each sentence.

1 As soon as they met again they hugged each ^~~another.~~ *other*
2 The company representative offered on paying for lunch.
3 No, we're just friends, we didn't go out in a date or anything like that.
4 You live near me so I'll take you up on the way, if you want.
5 I'm afraid I'll have to invite your kind invitation. I'll be holiday.
6 Little Johnny! Come and shake grandma on both cheeks!
7 It's not safe for you to walk round here at night. Don't worry, I'll pick you home.
8 Ronnie's so mean. He never even offers to paying when we go out.
9 Did you hear about that footballer who refused to shake arms before the game?
10 You don't have to pay just because you're a man. Let's shake the bill.

Listen and read

Culture clash

11a 🎧 **8.4 Listen and read the article. Put the items a–h in the order you hear them.**

a dress ☐
b time-keeping ☐
c translation problems ☐
d getting to know people personally ☐
e advertising and marketing a product 1
f calling people by their first names ☐
g business entertaining ☐
h giving gifts ☐

Sun	Mon	Tue	Wed	Thu	Fri	Sat
23	24	25	26	27	28	29
30	31	1	2	3	4	5
6	7	8	9	10	11	12
13	14	15	16	17	18	19
20	21	22	23	24	25	26
27	28	29	30	31	1	2

Culture Clash

In Africa, a famous food company tried to sell its baby food by advertising it with the picture of a baby on the label. They did not know that this particular country used labels only to show a picture of the food inside! When Pepsico used the slogan 'Come Alive With Pepsi' in Taiwan, they had no idea that it would be translated into Chinese as 'Pepsi brings your ancestors back from the dead'.

Misunderstandings such as these about language or about culture are sometimes comical but can also cause genuine hurt or anger. Business styles and customs vary widely in different countries and what is normal in one culture can be completely unacceptable in another. How well is your company prepared? Try this short test. Look at the following situations. What mistakes have been made?

1 You are in Paris on business. In a meeting it is very hot and you suggest to everyone that they take off their ties and roll up their sleeves.

2 A Japanese businessman asks, 'When do you want the report?' 'Yesterday!' answers the American businesswoman.

3 In an Arabic country, a group from a British company are invited to a dinner party. They all bring gifts and during the evening they continue to talk about their work.

4 A sales manager in Hong Kong is angry because his workers are always 15 minutes late for work. He makes a new rule that they all must come on time.

5 A Spanish secretary receives an urgent request to email a report to the New York office before 2 / 3. She sends it on 1st March.

6 You are having a meal with Chinese colleagues in Nanjing. After the meal you use the hot towel to wipe your hands and your face.

How did you do? Did you spot the 'cultural clashes'? Well, in the first situation, French businessmen rarely take off their ties even if the weather is very hot. The idea of the American 'casual Friday' where the boss is called by his or her first name and people can wear jeans and trainers is a complete mystery to many other nationalities. In Germany for example, colleagues often call each other by their titles and surnames, (e.g. Herr, Doktor) in the workplace.

For many Western countries, 'time is money' and good business equals fast business. However, in some cultures people consider that building good relationships with business partners is more important. They think in months and years and not days and hours and find Western executives impatient.

Socialising in different countries can be tricky. In Arabic countries, for example, people do not discuss business over meals. Giving gifts is another potential problem: in the UK most people take presents to a dinner party, but in many countries this is not polite because it suggests that you think the host is poor.

The Hong Kong story is true. The workers started coming on time but they also stopped exactly on time instead of working into the night as they used to do and left a great deal of work unfinished.

The Spanish secretary was a month late. She didn't realise that in America the month is written before the day, whereas in Europe the day comes first.

Finally, in the Chinese restaurant it is bad manners to wipe your face with a towel. Chinese people use it only for their hands.

So how did you do? Are you culturally aware or do you need a course in cross-cultural relationships? Whatever you do, remember that your way is not the only way and it is important to respect other people's customs.

b Listen and read again. Are the statements below true (T) or false (F)?

1 A famous company wanted to make food from babies. [F]
2 Cultural misunderstandings can often be funny. [ ]
3 French businessmen usually dress formally. [ ]
4 People usually call their boss by their first name in Germany. [ ]
5 In many Western countries, people don't like to waste time. [ ]
6 In Arab countries, there are special restaurants for discussing business plans. [ ]
7 In the UK, people bring presents to a party if the host is poor. [ ]
8 The Hong Kong workers did more work when they came in late. [ ]
9 In the USA, February 3rd can be written 2/3. [ ]
10 In Chinese restaurants, different towels are used to wipe your hands and your face. [ ]

Vocabulary

Talking about norms and customs

12 Use the prompts to make sentences about the advice in the article in exercise 11.

1 French businessmen / tend / keep their ties on.
French businessmen tend to keep their ties on.
2 In China / considered rude / use a hot towel to wipe your face.
____
3 Germans / not tend / call colleagues by their first names.
____
4 In Japan / good manners / build relationships slowly / doing business.
____
5 In many Arabic countries / unacceptable / talk about business during meals.
____
6 In the UK / important / take a gift to a dinner party.
____
7 In Spain / not usual / write 2nd July as 7/2.
____
8 In the USA / perfectly normal / people / wear casual clothes on Fridays.
____

13a Correct the mistakes in each sentence.

1 Men tend ^*to* shake hands when they meet and women tend to hug each other.
2 It's consider rude to show the bottom of your feet.
3 It's unaceptable to touch someone's head.
4 It's perfect normal to wear jeans in an office.
5 It's good manner to hold the door open for someone.
6 It's important saying sorry if you are in someone's way.
7 On the hole, it's OK to blow your nose in public.
8 On the whole, it's acceptable to men and women to share the bill when they go out.
9 Is bad manners to laugh without covering your mouth.
10 It's usually to take a present when you go to someone's house for dinner.

b Which sentences are true for your country? Change the ones which aren't to make them true.

09 STUFF!

Listen and read

eBay

1a 🎧 **9.1 Listen and read about eBay. Choose the best answers to complete the sentences.**

1 eBay is ______ .
  a a shop b a website c an office
2 The writer ______ things on eBay.
  a bought b found c sold
3 You can buy and sell ______ things on eBay.
  a lots of different b unusual c expensive
4 People ______ can use eBay.
  a in Europe b in the USA c all over the world

b Listen and read again and answer the questions.

1 You want to sell something on eBay. What three things do you have to do?

______

______

2 You want to buy the following things. Which category would you look in?
  a a ticket for the 2002 World Cup Final

  ______

  b a motorcycle

  ______

  c an apartment in Chicago

  ______

  d a pretty ornament of a cat

  ______

3 How did people find out about the company before 1996?

______

4 When did a lot of internet companies have problems?

______

5 Has eBay ever had any serious problems?

______

6 Who was the first Chief Executive Officer of eBay?

______

7 How does eBay make a profit?

______

8 Did the writer manage to sell everything?

______

Yesterday I cleared up my house and I mean *really* cleared up my house. The room that gave the most results was my husband's 'office'. There I found: one right-footed walking boot, size 10 (he lost the other one somewhere), a garden badminton set, complete with rackets and a net (we decided to get fit last summer and played with it once), a set of Star Wars videos and two small china cats someone gave me last birthday. I collected these and other 'finds', took them downstairs and logged on to www.eBay.com: the answer to all our rubbish – or 'one person's junk is another person's treasure.'

What is eBay? The simple answer is that it is the world's most popular auction house. The website says, 'eBay's mission is to provide a global trading platform where practically anyone can trade practically anything,' – yes, even one right-footed boot. People can sell and buy in a range of over 300 categories, including cars and other vehicles, movies and DVDs, sporting goods, collectibles, travel, tickets, musical instruments, real estate, clothes and shoes, jewellery – the list goes on and on.

The idea came from Peter Omidyar. Born in Paris, Omidyar, moved to Washington when he was still a child. At High School he became very interested in computer programming and after graduating from Tuft University

e-Reader

The online buyer's guide

in 1988, he worked for the next few years as a computer engineer. In his free time he started eBay as a kind of hobby, originally offering the service free by word of mouth. By 1996 there was so much traffic on the site that he had to upgrade and he began charging a fee to members. Joined by a friend, Peter Skoll, and in 1998 by his dynamic CEO, Meg Whitman, he has never looked back. Even in the great dot com crashes of the late 1990s eBay went from strength to strength. It is now one of the ten most visited online shopping sites on the internet.

If you think about it, it's a perfect internet idea. It sells connections not goods, putting buyer and seller into contact with each other. All you have to do is take an e-photo, write a description, fill out a sales form and you're in business; the world is your marketplace. Oh, and of course for each item sold, eBay gets a percentage and that is a great deal of money. Everyday there are more than 16 million items listed on eBay and 80 percent of items are sold.

Some of the more bizarre items up for offer have been a piece of French toast, partially eaten by Justin Timberlake, advertising space on a man's head, a pair of used false teeth, and 'Nothing' (the seller said he would give the profits to a local university).

One week later, I am the proud possessor of a clean and tidy home and £110 in cash. Someone even bought the boot.

Language focus 1

Defining relative clauses

2a **Match the sentence beginnings in A with the endings in B. Then complete the gaps with *who*, *which*, *whose* or *where*.**

A

1. A leisure time activity is something [c]
2. A determined person is someone [ ]
3. The Jim twins were brothers [ ]
4. An archaeological site is a place [ ]
5. A brilliant film is one [ ]
6. A confident person is someone [ ]
7. Kobe is the town in Japan [ ]
8. A disappointing book is one [ ]

B

a _____ people have found important historical buildings or objects.
b _____ believes in their own ability to do something.
c *which* you enjoy doing in your free time.
d _____ karaoke probably started.
e _____ knows what they want and works hard to get it.
f _____ we expect to be better than it is.
g _____ lives were remarkably similar.
h _____ people think is very good.

b 9.2 **Listen and check.**

3 **Read the conversation about holiday plans. Look at the relative pronouns in bold and bracket the ones which can be omitted.**

A: We're thinking of going to Spain this year. You went there last year, didn't you?

B: Yes, that's right. Actually I've got some photos (*which*) I can show you of where we went. It was Mohacar on the south coast. A friend **whose** daughter went there last year recommended it.

A: Oh, someone **who** I work with has been to Mohacar. It's a very quiet area, isn't it?

B: Yes, the thing **that** I liked most about it was the relaxing atmosphere. It's a place **where** you can forget all your problems.

A: How do you get there?

B: Well you can fly to Almeria, but that's quite expensive, or you can take any flight **which** goes to Malagar and drive east along the coast. I know several people **who** have done that. Anyway, do you want to see the photos?

4a **Look at the photos from Les's holiday last year. Les is talking about the photos. Join his sentences, using a relative pronoun.**

1

a This is the apartment. We rented it ...
This is the apartment which/that we rented

b ... and these are the people. They were staying in the apartment next door.
and these are the people who were staying in the apartment next door.

2

a This is the sea. We had breakfast there every morning ...

____

____

b ... and this is the beach. It was right in front of our apartment.

____

3

a This is a beach café. It stayed open till three in the morning ...

____

____

b ... and this is the man. He owned it.

____

____

4

a This is a fish restaurant. We had excellent meals there ...

____

b ... and this is a local woman. I can't remember her name.

____

5

a This is one day. We went on a boat trip ...

____

b ... and these are the men. We borrowed their boat.

____

6

a This is a market. It was open every Wednesday ...

____

b ... and this is me wearing a hat. I bought it there.

____

b **Look again at your sentences in exercise 4a and bracket the relative pronoun if it can be omitted.**

Vocabulary

How gadgets work

5a **Complete the conversations with the correct form of the words/phrases in the box.**

~~crashed~~	scroll down	hold down	switch off
break down	recharge	restart	
touch (the) icon		reinstall (the)software	
unplug	(not) work	press	

A **A:** Good morning, Patricia speaking. How can I help?
B: Hello. I've got a problem with my tablet computer. I was working on a document this morning and it [1]*crashed* three times.
A: Have you tried [2]________ it?
B: Yes, several times.
A: OK, well I think the best thing to do is [3]________ the ________. First, you need to ...

B **A:** Good morning, Meccaphone, George speaking.
B: Hi! I hope you can help. My touch-screen phone's gone dead.
A: How long have you had it?
B: A week.
A: You probably need to [4]________ the battery.
B: And another thing ... I can't access the apps I've downloaded.
A: You need to access the downloads folder. Open 'settings' and [5]________ ________ the menu with your finger until you come to 'downloads'. Then [6]________ the ________ and they should be there.
B: OK, thanks!

C **A:** Good morning, Print Logistics. How can I help you?
B: Morning. Our photocopier [7]________. Every time we try to copy something, it [8]________ and stops working.
A: OK, [9]________ it ________ at the wall, then [10]________ it.
B: Hang on ... oh, right, I've done that.
A: [11]________ ________ the 'print' button while you switch it back on. Can you see a menu?
B: Yes, I see it.
A: In the menu, [12]________ 'restart'. That should solve the problem.

b **9.3 Listen and check.**

Pronunciation

Stress patterns in compound nouns

6a **Complete the table with the compound nouns in the box.**

~~digital camera~~	~~laptop~~
internet addict	dishwasher
bodyguard	personal trainer
electric cooker	recycling bin
energy drink	personal computer
instruction manual	washing machine
mobile phone	games console

Stress on the first part	Stress on both parts
•	• •
laptop	*digital camera*

b **9.4 Listen and check.**

Language focus 2

Quantifiers

7a **Are the words in the box countable or uncountable? If they are countable, are they singular or plural? Write them in the table.**

~~banana~~	chair	children	fruit	
information	jewellery	milk	money	news
people	person	petrol	pollution	
potatoes	price	rice	ring	storm
sugar	traffic	vegetable	weather	

countable singular	*banana*
countable plural	
uncountable	

b **Choose the correct answers.**

1 The children ***is*** / ***are*** upstairs.
2 The fruit ***isn't*** / ***aren't*** ready to eat yet.
3 The weather ***was*** / ***were*** very bad.
4 Who ***is*** / ***are*** the people behind you in the photo?
5 Petrol ***is*** / ***are*** getting more and more expensive.
6 How much money ***is*** / ***are*** there in my account?
7 ***Is*** / ***Are*** the jewellery real?
8 The traffic ***was*** / ***were*** terrible.
9 I'm afraid there ***is*** / ***are*** no news yet.
10 The information ***was*** / ***were*** wrong.

8a Sandra is trying to persuade Aileen to go to a party but Aileen doesn't want to go. Match Aileen's comments 1–7 with a response from Sandra a–g. Then complete the sentences with the words in the box.

~~anything~~	~~some~~	enough	few	got	have
lots of	many	much	no	isn't	of
plenty	couple				

Aileen:

1 I haven't got *anything* to wear. [e]
2 I've got ____________ friends. [ ]
3 I haven't ____________ much money. [ ]
4 There'll be too ____________ people. [ ]
5 I never ____________ anything to say. [ ]
6 I've got too ____________ homework to do. [ ]
7 There ____________ enough time to get ready. [ ]

Sandra:

a You've got a ____________ of hours tomorrow when you could finish it.
b There's ____________ time – we don't need to be there until nine!
c Don't be silly. You've got ____________ you could talk about.
d Come on ... you've got loads ____________ friends.
e But you've got *some* really nice clothes.
f You only need ____________ for a taxi.
g Oh, but only a ____________ people are coming.

b 9.5 Listen and check.

9 Find and correct the mistake in each sentence.

1 Now my father is retired he's got plenty ^ *of* time for his hobby: surfing the internet.
2 I think the soup needs a few salt. It doesn't have much taste.
3 There were too many people and too many noise, so Jan couldn't see or hear the prime minister.
4 I don't think there's enough of food for 100 people.
5 Lisbon has got loads of good shops but there's not much of parking space in the city centre.
6 There are plenty of tickets left for the afternoon performance, but no many for the evening.
7 I want to thank everyone who has given me a lot support.
8 There are plenty things to eat, so please help yourself.
9 We've got lot of friends who live nearby.
10 We haven't got some milk in the fridge.
11 There were loads things to do before the party started; fortunately David helped.
12 Sorry, but I can't go on holiday with you. I've got none money.

Vocabulary
Describing everyday objects

10 Use *they're both, they're both made of, they've both got* or *they're both used for* and a word in the box to write a description for each pair 1–8.

~~leather~~	batteries	rectangular	round	metal
glass	sticking	wool		

1 shoes and handbags
They're both made of leather.
2 a window and a wine bottle
____
3 a knife and scissors
____
4 a towel and a book
____
5 sellotape and glue
____
6 an alarm clock and portable speakers
____
7 a ring and a plate
____
8 a jumper and a scarf
____

Language live

Buying things

11a Put the words in the correct order to make questions.

1 help / I / Can / all / at ?
Can I help at all?
2 to / How / pay / like / would / you ?
____
3 if / I / Can / right / isn't / back / it / bring / it ?
____
4 those / get / How / with / on / you / did ?
____
5 for / to / delivery / I / Do / pay / have ?
____
6 product / Have / code / a / got / you ?
____
7 this / have / 16 / Do / size / a / you / in ?
____
8 including / that / VAT / Is ?
____

b Match the questions 1–8 with the responses a–h.

a No, you don't. Orders over £50 are delivered free. [5]
b Yes, they were OK. [ ]
c No, thanks. I'm just looking [ ]
d Yes, that's fine. Just keep your receipt. [ ]
e No, it's not. [ ]
f I'll have a look for you. [ ]
g By credit card, please. [ ]
h Yes, it's XU319. [ ]

c 9.6 Listen and check.

Writing

Formal and informal styles

12a Look at the two letters about things which have been lost. A is informal and B is more formal. Complete the letters with the phrases in the box.

~~Just writing to say~~
I don't suppose you've found it
I do hope it has been found
could you post it
I would be grateful if you could send it
let me know how much the postage is
I will of course pay for postage
I am writing to enquire whether

A

46 Broom Way
23rd February

Dear Andy,

[1]*Just writing to say* thanks again for having us last weekend. We both had a really good time.

The only thing is, I've lost one of my earrings: I know I was wearing it on Sunday and when we got home, I couldn't find it. Perhaps it fell off while I was playing with the children in the garden.

[2]____________ ?

I don't know if you remember it. It's quite big, made of silver, with a blue stone set in it. The earrings are quite special to me because they were a birthday present from Peter.

If you do happen to find it, [3]____________ to me? Obviously, [4]____________. Anyway, I'll keep my fingers crossed!

Lots of love,

Ingrid

B

22 Prince Avenue,
Horbury

The Manager,
Sherbon Hotel,
Vermont

27th March

Dear Sir / Madam,

[5]____________ you have found a camera which I left in my hotel room last weekend. I was staying in room 201 from 21st–23rd. I am almost certain that I left the camera in the bedside cabinet.

[6]____________ since it is a very expensive model. It is a Nikon compact, in a black leather case with a red and black strap.

[7]____________ by registered post to the above address. [8]____________.

Yours faithfully,
Ian Crompton

b Imagine that you have just finished a language course in the UK, and you realise that you have left something in a classroom. Write to the school to ask about it. The address is: Success Language School, Dewbury Road, Brighton.

10 SOCIETY AND CHANGE

Vocabulary
Numbers and statistics

1 a 10.1 Listen and choose the number you hear. Then listen again and repeat the numbers.

1	(16%)	60%
2	15,025	50,025
3	1.5 million	1.5 billion
4	13°C	30 C
5	1,045 km^2	1,450 km^2
6	a profit of 20%	a profit of 21%

b Write the numbers in full.

1 47% *forty-seven percent*
2 $12,265 ________
3 15 m^2 ________
4 €305,000 ________
5 30°C ________
6 70 kph ________
7 10,000,000 ________
8 4.3 ________

Language focus 1
Making predictions

2 Put *will ('ll)* or *won't* in the best place in the sentences.

1 Don't worry. I ^forget! (*won't*)
2 Why don't you buy Meg this bag? She love it!
3 I know I win but I buy a lottery ticket every week.
4 Let me make a photocopy. It take long.
5 There be lots of food at the party.
6 The flight takes two hours, so you arrive at 10 o'clock.
7 Don't panic. The coach go without you!
8 I'm going to the conference in Lisbon. You be there?
9 It definitely rain this afternoon. You can leave your umbrella at home.
10 You probably have to wait a long time, so take a book with you.

3 Complete the sentences with *is/are/isn't/aren't likely to* and the verb in brackets.

1 You *'re likely to find* (find) the food strange at first.
2 We ________ (not eat) until late, so have something now if you're hungry.
3 Rooney ________ (not play) on Saturday.
4 The news ________ (be) bad. They think a lot of people were hurt.
5 You ________ (not improve) if you don't practise.
6 We ________ (sleep) much tonight. They're having a party next door.
7 Passengers ________ (experience) long delays at the airport.
8 Graeme and Shirley ________ (not arrive) here soon, what with all this traffic.
9 Jo ________ (have) a great time on holiday. She certainly deserves a rest.
10 The weather ________ (get) worse, so bring an umbrella.

4a Complete the answers with *may well* and a verb in the box.

~~find~~ cancel fail get married leave snow

1 **A:** I've never done any salsa dancing before.
B: In that case, you *may well find* it best to take some lessons.
2 **A:** Melanie seems unhappy in her job.
B: Yes. She ________________ the company soon.
3 **A:** How long have Jon and Sylvie been going out with each other?
B: Almost a year now and they ________________ next year.
4 **A:** I am phoning to check my flight. It's BA 2517.
B: Conditions are very poor at the moment and they ________________ the flight.
5 **A:** When is your driving test?
B: In two days' time. I feel OK about the practical but I ________________ the written exam.
6 **A:** It's very cold, isn't it? Have you seen the weather forecast today?
B: Yes. It ________________ later.

b 10.2 **Listen and check.**

5 **Put the words in the correct order. The first word is underlined.**

1 tonight / see / I'll / definitely / Ray
I'll definitely see Ray tonight.
2 probably / pass / Carlos / his / exam / won't
____
3 stay / New York / decide / in / Teresa / may / to / well
____
4 get / isn't / to / Sandy / job / likely / the
____
5 next / almost / I'll / computing / year / do / certainly / a / course
____
6 so / could / us / late / don't / We / for / wait / be
____
7 weekend / away / probably / We / this / go / won't
____
8 loads / are / on / There / the / likely / beach / be / to / people / of
____
9 won't / Jamie / test / his / certainly / pass / almost
____
10 more / humans / are / Robots / than / intelligent / unlikely / become / to
____

6a **Rewrite these sentences so that they mean the same, using the words in brackets.**

1 Brazil are likely to win the World Cup.
Brazil *may well win the* World Cup. (may well)
2 I'm sure we won't have time to do any sightseeing.
We ________________ (definitely)
3 It'll probably rain before the end of the day.
It ________________ (likely)
4 Perhaps my friend Mari will be a famous actress one day.
My friend Mari ________________ (could)
5 My boss is very unlikely to agree to the pay rise.
My boss ________________ (almost certainly)
6 I think you'll recognise my sister when you see her.
You ________________ (probably)
7 We probably won't get back from the theatre before midnight.
We ________________ (likely)
8 I'm sure that our teacher will give us a lot of homework for the weekend.________________
Our teacher ________________ (almost certainly)

b 10.3 **Listen to the sentences and change them, using the prompts given.**

You hear:

Brazil are likely to win the World Cup. (may well)

You say:

Brazil may well win the World Cup.

Vocabulary
Society and change

7a Write ↑ or ↓.

1 become more (+ adjective) ↑
2 decrease ____
3 go up ____
4 get better ____
5 fall ____
6 become less (+ adjective) ____
7 increase ____
8 deteriorate ____
9 get worse ____
10 go down ____
11 improve ____
12 rise ____

b Complete the newspaper articles with the phrases from exercise 7a. (More than one phrase is possible in each case.)

UK divorce rate improves

The number of people who get divorced has [1] *decreased / fallen / gone down* to a ten-year low according to the Office for National Statistics. There were 144,600 divorces last year compared with 158,000 ten years ago. It is the third year that the number of divorces has [2] ____________ . Unfortunately, however, getting divorced is becoming a habit. The number of people divorcing for the second or third time has [3] ____________ sharply. It is now almost double the number of ten years ago.

Equality at work?

The number of working women has [4] ____________ dramatically in the last 50 years. In 1960 one in four married women went out to work. Today, nearly three out of four do so.
However, most employees in the lowest-paid professions are women. Their conditions of work have not [5] ____________ much, and it is normal to work long hours for minimum pay. In some cases, in fact, the conditions have [6] ____________ since the 1960s, with employers demanding longer hours at difficult times. To balance this, it has [7] ____________ easier for women to climb to the top of their profession and the number of female managers, directors, top lawyers and doctors is significantly greater.

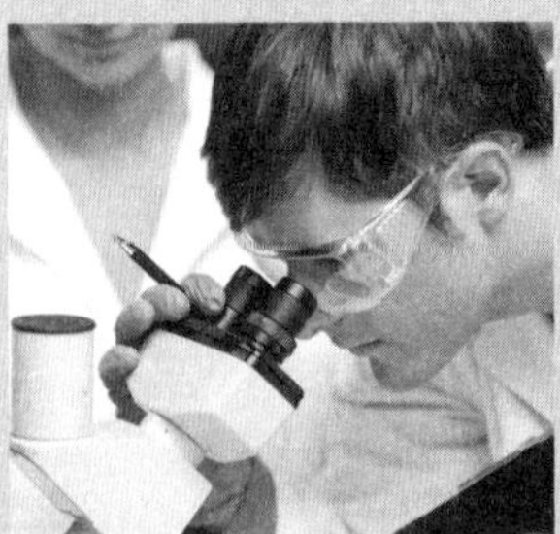

Geniuses should not get married

Geniuses should not get married, according to Dr Satoshi Kanazawa of New Zealand. Male scientists tend to have their biggest successes before their mid-30s and after that their ability to invent or discover something important rapidly [8] ____________ . Just like male birds and animals, young men are competitive and want to attract females; their creativity [9] ____________ during their 20s and 30s, but as soon as they get married and have families, it begins to disappear.

Language focus 2
Hypothetical possibilities with *if*

8a Complete the questions about imaginary situations with the correct form of the verbs in brackets.

1 If you *won* (win) a lot of money, what *would* you *do* (do) with it?
2 What ____________ you ____________ (do) if someone ____________ (try) to rob you in the street?
3 If you ____________ (break down) on the motorway, ____________ you ____________ (get out) of the car?
4 ____________ you ____________ (know) what to do if someone ____________ (cut) their arm badly?
5 If you ____________ (know) a friend of yours was stealing money from his company, ____________ you ____________ (tell) anyone?
6 ____________ you ____________ (feel) safe walking home alone at night in your town?
7 ____________ you ever ____________ (move) to another country if you ____________ (have) the chance?
8 ____________ you ever ____________ (eat) raw meat?
9 What ____________ you ____________ (do) if you ____________ (find) out you were going to have a baby?
10 If someone ____________ (offer) you a free bungee jump, what ____________ you ____________ (do)?

b **Match answers a–j with the questions in exercise 8a.**

- **a** If I was hungry enough, yes, I would. ☐
- **b** I think I'd probably tie something round it. ☐
- **c** Oh yes, I'd love to have the opportunity to experience another culture. ☐
- **d** No, I wouldn't. I'd lock the doors and stay inside. ☐
- **e** I might do it for the experience if I was feeling brave! ☐
- **f** I'd cry with happiness and tell all my family! ☐
- **g** I might tell another friend so we could decide what to do. ☐
- **h** I'd probably just give him all my money and run. ☐
- **i** No, I definitely wouldn't. It's too dangerous after dark here. ☐
- **j** I'd travel round the world. 1

c **What would you do in the situations in exercise 8a. Write your answers using *I'd, I wouldn't, I might, I could*.**

1 ______
2 ______
3 ______
4 ______
5 ______
6 ______
7 ______
8 ______
9 ______
10 ______

9a **Complete the conversations with the correct form of the verb in brackets.**

A **A:** I can't decide whether to have the baby in hospital or not.
B: Well, I [1] *'d go* (go) into hospital, especially as it's your first baby.
A: Yes, you're probably right.
B: Have you decided on a name yet?
A: Yes – if it [2] ______ (be) a boy, we [3] ______ (call) him Tom, and if it [4] ______ (be) a girl, Sara.

B **A:** Why aren't you going to your classes?
B: Because they're so boring: I [5] ______ (go) if they [6] ______ (be) more interesting. And I always get bad marks.
A: Well, that's not surprising: if you [7] ______ (spend) less time playing computer games and [8] ______ (work) harder, you [9] ______ (not have) so many problems.

b **10.4 Listen and check.**

10 **Use the correct form of the word/phrases in the box to complete the sentences below.**

~~retire early~~ take the day off work
trust your more live
take revenge not be cheap
be taller start a business
be on fire worry less about my health

1 If I were rich, *I'd retire early*.
2 If Rodrigo lost his job, ______.
3 James could go on that ride ______.
4 She would tell you her secret ______.
5 If someone did something really bad to you, ______?
6 If I were ill, ______.
7 I might throw water over my bed ______!
8 If you could live in another country, where ______?
9 We wouldn't go to this restaurant ______.
10 If I could live forever, ______.

Pronunciation
'll or *'d* in connected speech

11a **10.5 Listen and write the six sentences you hear.**

1 *I'd move to Antarctica if* ______
2 ______
3 ______
4 ______
5 ______
6 ______

b **Finish the sentences so they are true for you.**

Listen and read

Stuck on a desert island?

12a 🎧 **10.6 Listen and read the website discussion and answer the questions.**

1 Who would be lonely?

____

2 Who would not enjoy the silence?

____

3 Who would miss food or drink?

____

4 Who would hate being on a desert island?

____

talkingpoints.com

HOME | LATEST | PREVIOUS CHATS

Stuck on a desert island?

STARTED ON 23RD AUGUST BY STEVE 2

POSTS 1–7 OF 42

POST 1 **STEVE, USA**

Hi everyone,
What would you miss most and least if you were stuck on a desert island? For me it would be the changing seasons, especially the fall in New England. Sure, it would be fantastic to have non-stop sun, but I'd miss the colours of the seasons. I guess this will sound stupid but I'd probably miss the rain too! I wouldn't miss getting up at six every day to go to work, though! What about you?

POST 2 **TOMAS, GERMANY**

Good question, Steve. I think I'd miss the pastries and different types of bread, and shopping at the local markets, and sausages, although I suppose I could try and make my own. So, yeah, the food. I'd miss the food most. What would I miss least? My mobile – I'd like to be completely uncontactable – at least for a little while.

POST 3 **PAOLA, ITALY**

I would miss the company of people because I know I'd like to have someone to share experiences with. For instance, if there was a fantastic sunrise I'd want someone to be there to enjoy it with me. I'm a sociable sort of person and I'd go mad on my own. And I definitely wouldn't miss junk mail – I hate coming home every evening and finding a pile of junk mail in my post box.

POST 4 **MIKO, JAPAN**

Hi,
I would miss Manga cartoons, the internet and Japanese food, like nori, sushi and Japanese beef. I'd also miss TV shows and shopping for clothes ... and my two dogs. In fact, I'd miss everything.

POST 5 **ROGER, UK**

I would miss my daily newspaper and listening to the news on the TV and radio. I'd feel very cut off if I didn't know what was happening in the world. If you gave me a radio, then I'd be perfectly happy to live on a desert island for the rest of my life. What I'd miss least would be traffic jams in the city, particularly my journey to work.

POST 6 **JAYNE, CANADA**

Why hasn't anyone mentioned their family? I'd be lost without my husband and two kids. They're the most important things for me. Maybe coffee, too. I can't get started in the morning without a cup of black coffee. I wouldn't miss doing the housework. Just think, no more cleaning or washing-up! And it'd be good to be able to relax as much as I wanted.

POST 7 **JAIME, MEXICO**

It would have to be music. I couldn't live without my music!

I wouldn't miss going to school at all or doing homework!

b Are these statements true (T) or false (F)?

1 Steve would be bored by too much sunny weather. ☐
2 Tomas would probably hate being alone. ☐
3 Nobody would miss living in a city. ☐
4 Paola hates getting letters. ☐
5 Three people would miss technology. ☐
6 Jaime enjoys school. ☐

Vocabulary

Society

13 **Complete the definitions with words in the box.**

~~pollution~~	homelessness
corruption	unemployment
wealthy	tax-payers
racism	healthcare
poor	education

1 *pollution* : dirty air, water, etc.
2 ________ : very rich
3 ________ : teaching and learning in school or university
4 ________ : being without a place to live
5 ________ : service provided by doctors, hospitals, etc.
6 ________ : being without a job
7 ________ : people who work and pay money to the government
8 ________ : dishonest behaviour
9 ________ : believing that other groups of people are different and not as good as your own
10 ________ : having little money

14 **Choose the correct answers to complete the sentences.**

1 ***Homelessness*** / ***Pollution*** has increased as more people are living on the street.
2 It's difficult to vote nowadays as ***ordinary people*** / ***the opposition parties*** are so similar to the government.
3 Since the start of the war more money has been spent on ***tax-payers*** / ***defence***.
4 The government shouldn't ***waste money on*** / ***reduce spending on*** improving parks when we have more serious problems.
5 Hospitals have improved a lot since the government made ***education*** / ***healthcare*** a priority.
6 The scandal involving the minister was just another example of the ***pollution*** / ***corruption*** common in politics.
7 I think the government should ***reduce taxes for*** / ***waste money on*** people in key jobs: teachers, doctors, etc.
8 People were angry when they discovered the president had used ***tax payers'*** / ***the opposition parties'*** money to pay for his holiday.
9 ***Crime*** / ***Unemployment*** has reached 30 percent, which means that 3 out of 10 people don't have a job.
10 I hate ***racism*** / ***corruption***. How can you judge someone by the colour of their skin?
11 I think ***the wealthy*** / ***the poor*** should pay more tax, as they have more money.
12 The government's new 'clean-air' law aims to reduce ***pollution*** / ***unemployment*** in big cities.

11 RULES

Language focus 1
Obligation and permission in the present

1a Rewrite the sentences, replacing the words in bold with the correct form of *is/are allowed to*.

1 You **can't** eat in here.
You aren't allowed to eat in here.
2 You **can** walk on the grass.
____
3 **Is it OK for us** to use a calculator?
____
4 Visitors **must not** touch the exhibits.
____
5 On Saturdays, we **can** stay up until ten o'clock.
____
6 Children under five **cannot** use the swimming pool without an adult.
____
7 **Can I** hang pictures on the walls?
____
8 **It's OK for you to** wear casual clothes.
____
9 You **mustn't** use your mobile phone in here.
____
10 **Can we** take photos in here?
____

b Choose the correct alternative in each sentence.

1 You ***should*** / ***are allowed to*** get more exercise. You're not very healthy.
2 You ***can*** / ***mustn't*** register online or by phone, it's up to you.
3 Our teacher's very strict. We ***aren't allowed to*** / ***can*** speak unless we raise our hand first.
4 Candidates ***must*** / ***are allowed to*** present photo ID at the start of the exam.
5 You ***don't have to*** / ***shouldn't*** talk to her like that, it's rude.
6 You ***don't have to*** / ***mustn't*** make notes, but you can if you want to.
7 Passengers ***ought to*** / ***mustn't*** distract the driver when the bus is moving.
8 You ***ought to*** / ***are allowed to*** let him know if you're going to be late.
9 People in my country ***are allowed to*** / ***can't*** get married until they are 18.
10 Residents ***shouldn't*** / ***are allowed to*** keep pets, but only a cat or dog.

2a Complete the sentences with the words in the box.

~~have~~	should	mustn't	can
can't	must	ought	don't have
are allowed	aren't allowed		

1 You *have* to leave your keys at reception when you go out of the hotel.
2 I think people ____________ spend more time with their families and less time at work.
3 Passengers ____________ to walk around the plane when it is taking off.
4 Candidates ____________ to take a dictionary into the exam, but they can't take in a grammar book.
5 You ____________ drive a car unless you're over 17.
6 You look really tired. I think you ____________ to take a day off.
7 Monday's a holiday so we ____________ to go to school until Tuesday.
8 You ____________ ride a bicycle on the motorway – it's very dangerous.
9 Guests ____________ have breakfast any time between 7 and 9 a.m.
10 You ____________ sign your name in this book when you enter or leave the building.

b 11.1 Listen and check. Then practise saying the sentences, paying attention to the weak forms.

3 Here are the answers to some questions about rules. First decide if they are about a language class (LC), a library (LIB) or a sports club (SC). Then use the prompts to make complete questions.

1 You can borrow four books at a time. _LIB_
How many books / allowed / borrow / at a time?
How many books am I allowed to borrow at a time?

2 Yes, you can book two days in advance. ___
Can / book / aerobics classes in advance?
______________________________________?

3 You're allowed to keep them for a week. ____
How long / allowed / keep books?
__________________________?

4 Yes, first you take a short written test, then there's an interview with a teacher. ____
Have to / take a test?
______________________________________?

5 Yes, bring a passport-sized photo for your membership card. ____
Should / bring a photo?
______________________________________?

6 Well, if you miss too many, you won't get a certificate at the end of the course. ____
How many classes / allowed / miss?
______________________________________?

Pronunciation
Modal verbs in connected speech

4a 11.2 Modal verbs in connected speech.

1 _You can't park there._
2 ______________________________
3 ______________________________
4 ______________________________
5 ______________________________
6 ______________________________
7 ______________________________
8 ______________________________

b Listen again. Practise saying the sentences.

Vocabulary
Linking words

5 Read the text and choose the correct linking words.

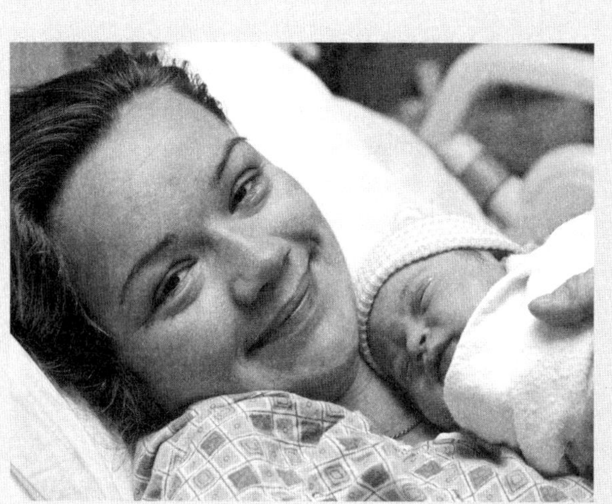

Nowadays, science has made it possible for a couple who can't have children to pay a woman to have their baby for them. These 'surrogate' mothers sign a contract promising to give the baby to the couple as soon as it is born, in return for a large sum of money. [1]***However*** / ***Also***, this business arrangement does not always work well in practice and, [2]***despite this*** / ***as a result***, there have been a number of 'horror stories' in the newspapers recently.

People have strong feelings on both sides. Some say that it is every woman's right to have a child. [3]***Although*** / ***What is more***, a surrogate mother can often save an unhappy marriage and make some money for herself. [4]***Therefore*** / ***Despite this***, many people are against this practice. They say that [5]***although*** / ***besides*** they understand the heartache of a childless woman, having a baby is not an automatic right. They feel the whole thing is completely unnatural and [6]***for this reason*** / ***also*** should not be allowed. [7]***Besides*** / ***However***, they ask what will happen to the child when he or she is old enough to know the truth. This could have a terrible effect on their mental and emotional development. I feel that this last point is particularly important and, [8]***therefore*** / ***what is more***, I tend to agree that surrogacy is wrong, or at least that there should be stricter rules about it.

Vocabulary
Crime and punishment

6 Choose the correct answers.

1 The *murderer* was sentenced to life imprisonment.
   a murder   b murderer   c murdered
2 When they received the phone call, they knew their daughter had been ________
   a kidnapping   b kidnapper   c kidnapped
3 The ________ took place at 3:15 p.m. in the Arnos Road branch of the bank.
   a robbery   b robber   c robbed
4 When the staff found the stolen camera in his bag, Dave was arrested for ________
   a shoplifting   b shoplifter   c shoplifted
5 The old lady was ________ as she walked home on her own.
   a mugging   b mugger   c mugged
6 As they sorted through the mess, Judy realised the ________ had taken her favourite necklace.
   a burglary   b burglars   c burgled
7 When the police discovered his alibi was false, he was ________ for murder.
   a arrest   b arrested   c catch

Language focus 2
Obligation and permission in the past

7 Paolo has just finished his military service abroad and is talking about the rules and regulations in the army. Put the sentences into the past.

1 I have to get up at 5:30 a.m.
   I had to get up at 5:30 a.m.
2 I must clean my boots everyday.
   ____
3 I'm not allowed to have long hair.
   ____
4 I can't email home.
   ____
5 We can watch a movie every Saturday evening.
   ____
6 We are allowed go into town once a month.
   ____
7 I don't have to pay for my meals.
   ____

8 Put the words in the correct order to make conversations. The first word is underlined.

A **A:** exam / to / calculator / Were / a / allowed / the / take / into / you ?
   1 *Were you allowed to take a calculator into the exam?*
B: weren't / No / we
   2 ________
A: did / answer / many / have / How / questions / to / you ?
   3 ________
B: three / We / do / in / had / hours / twenty / to
   4 ________

B **A:** up / allowed / you / late / to / Were / stay ?
   1 ________
B: campfire / we / by / midnight / Yeah / until / sit / the / could
   2 ________
A: get / early / you / up / Did / to / have ?
   3 ________
B: to / nine / we / No / up / didn't / until / get / have
   4 ________

C **A:** Australia / a / Did / have / Francoise / time / in / good ?
   1 ________
B: six / week / to / she / work / No / a / days / had
   2 ________
B: terrible / That's !
   3 ________
A: allowed / us / to / wasn't / she / phone / And
   4 ________

9 Complete the sentences with the words in the box.

must	mustn't (x2)	have to
don't have to (x2)	had to	didn't have to

1 You *mustn't* use your mobile phone in the library.
2 It's free to get in: you ________ pay.
3 I missed my train and I ________ wait half an hour for the next one.
4 It's not a direct flight to New Zealand: you ________ change planes at Bangkok.
5 There were only two people in front of me in the queue so I ________ wait long.
6 Don't cry, Jessica – you ________ play with Jon if you don't want to.
7 You ________ walk on the railway line.
8 I ________ remember to post this letter.

Listen and read

Children sue parents

10a 11.3 Listen to and read the four newspaper stories and answer the questions.

1 Who wanted separation from their parents?

______

2 Who did not like the way their child looked?

______

3 Who liked the way their child looked?

______

4 Who had an accident?

______

5 Who was afraid of one of their parents?

______

6 Who was not in control of their own money?

______

7 Who had a famous son or daughter?

______

8 Who was successful in suing their parents?

______

b Match the numbers with the things they refer to.

1 5 ☐
2 1,000 ☐
3 2 ☐
4 15 ☐
5 1996 ☐

a the number of years the father had been telling the child to do something
b the age the child was when he sued
c the number of jars of cookies
d the year the child left home
e the amount paid for damages

1 When 15-year-old Mario Silva refused to cut his hair because he wanted to look like his favourite film star, his father pulled out a gun and threatened to shoot him. 'My husband had been telling Mario to get his hair cut for the last two years and they had an argument,' said his wife. Fernando Silva was arrested and will appear in court next week. Meanwhile Mario has decided to sue him and to ask to be formally separated from his parents. 'I don't feel safe in the house anymore,' he told our reporter.

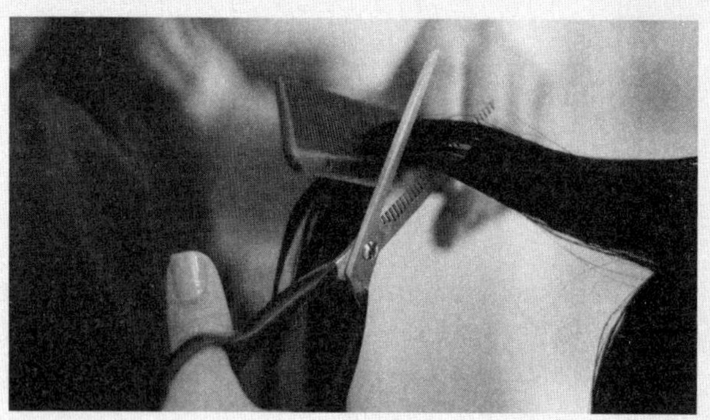

2 A Jamaican woman sued her parents after falling down the stairs of their home during a visit. Beatrice, who was in her early 20s, said that her parents had been negligent because they 'failed to look after the carpet on the stairs.' As a result of the fall, she suffered serious and permanent injuries when she tripped over the carpet in August 2002. She was awarded $1,000 in damages at a court in Kingston.

3 In 1996, 17-year-old Olympic gold medallist Dominique Moceneau left home and asked to become a legal adult and to be in control of her own money. She said that her father, Dumitru Moceneau, had taken all her winnings and left her with no money and that her parents had robbed her of her childhood by pushing her so hard to become a gymnast. After hearing her complaints, a Texan court granted her independence from her parents.

4 A Canadian actress is suing her parents for making her fat. Tina Stowe, a well-known TV star in Canada, says that her mother, Lisa, kept five jars of cookies in the house in places where a child could easily find them and used to make the situation worse by telling her she was prettier than the other girls in her school. Stowe has said that her mother should have married a more suitable partner, preferably someone of a slimmer build. Stowe will appear in court next month.

Language live

Expressing and responding to opinions

11a Put the words in the correct order to complete the conversations.

1 **A:** Children have an easy life these days.
B: say / that / do / why / you ?
Why do you say that?

2 **A:** People who get caught shoplifting should be sent to prison.
B: that / know / I / don't / about / my / opinion / In
____
it depends on what they steal.

3 **A:** It seems to me that people who come from broken families usually become criminals.
B: Well, / your / take / I / point
____
It's sometimes true, but / honest / be / really / to / agree / I / don't
____
There are lots of examples where the opposite is true.

4 **A:** I think he's innocent.
B: mean / do / What / you ?
____
He was caught on camera!

5 **A:** In my opinion, prison never works as a punishment.
B: It *never* works?
remember / to / You / have / that
____
in some cases it's the only option to protect the public.

6 **A:** What do you think about this new law on immigration?
B: you / I / know / about / don't / I / but / think
____
it's a bit harsh.

b 11.4 **Listen and check. Practise saying the phrases.**

12a Match the newspaper headlines 1–3 with extracts A–C.

1

SMOKING TO BE BANNED IN PUBLIC PARKS

2

TAX INCREASES FOR THE WEALTHY

3

CELEBRITY SAYS PRESS HAS TOO MUCH FREEDOM

A

The government is to announce a range of measures to increase tax rates for the wealthiest 20 percent today.

Speaking at a press conference, new Minister of Finance Jerry Holdwell said, "For too long the wealthiest 20 percent have avoided paying more tax in this country, while the poorest members of society find it difficult to meet their everyday living costs."

B

UPDATE

Daffyd Evans, the Welsh singer, is the latest celebrity to speak out over the tabloid press, following the recent privacy scandals involving several UK newspapers. Speaking in an interview for a music programme, he said, "Although I agree with freedom of the press, when 'journalists' sit in a car outside my house watching me, and I have to keep my curtains closed, I think freedom has gone too far."

C

NEWS

Life is about to get even more difficult for smokers in New York, after Ed O'Brien, current mayor of New York, has announced a new municipal law to ban smoking in public parks. Anti-smoking campaigners have welcomed the law, saying it will allow families to enjoy nature in a clean, smoke-free environment.

b Use the words in the box to complete the conversations.

~~to~~ don't	honest	In	but
about	take	mean	

1 **A:** You have [1] *to* remember that it's a journalist's job to uncover people's secrets.
B: What do you [2] ________ ? Surely their stories should be in the public interest?

2 **A:** [3] ________ my opinion this is an excellent idea. They just ruin the air for everyone else.
B: I don't know [4] ________ that. They're outside and this is going a bit too far.

3 **A:** I [5] ________ know about you, [6] ________ I think if they've worked hard they deserve their money.
B: Well, I [7] ________ your point but to be [8] ________ I don't really agree. These people are just born into money.

c Match each conversation with the news stories in exercise 12a.

Conversation 1: ________
Conversation 2: ________
Conversation 3: ________

Writing

Checking for mistakes

13 Here is an opinion essay on restorative justice. The teacher has marked the mistakes using the following code. Look at the code and correct the mistakes.

^	for a missing word
sp	for spelling
wo	for word order
vf	for verb form
ww	for wrong word

Restorative justice should be used more often as a form of punishment. Discuss.

sp Restorative justice is a form of punishment for certain crimes (usually ^ ~~voilent~~ violent crimes or theft),
vf where the victim has the opportunity met the criminal who committed the crime, and explain the effect
ww that it had on them. It is many used in exchange for shorter prison sentences,
^ and some people argue that should be used more often as it forces the criminals to face up to the effects
vf of what they doing. In my opinion, it is an effective punishment which should be used more often.

sp Fistly, in the few cases where it has been used so far, it has a proven success rate.
^ Most criminals have taken part in the process do not return to crime when they are released from
wo prison. More is what, it gives the victims a chance to explain how they felt when the crime happened and
ww how it has affected their lives. For that because, the victim can actually see justice being done.

wo However, there are some arguments important against more common use of restorative justice.
sp For example, many poeple argue that it is a 'soft' option, and that criminals only have to have one or
vf two meetings then they are free committing more crimes. They also argue that it creates
sp unneccesary further stress for the victim, since they have to face up to the person who caused them pain.

^ Despite this, I strongly believe that in most cases, restorative justice a highly effective punishment in
ww preventing criminals for repeating their crimes. I am therefore convinced that it should be used more often.

12 YOUR CHOICE

Language focus 1

could have, should have, would have

1 **Look at pictures A–F and match them with captions 1–6 below.**

1 'Oh well, they wouldn't have had room for my luggage, anyway.' ☐
2 'What do you mean, you gave him your sweets? I'd have hit him.' ☐
3 'Darling, you could have hurt yourself.' ☐
4 'Oh well, it's not too bad – we could have lost everything.' ☐
5 'I knew I shouldn't have gone to that hairdresser.' ☐
6 'You should have told me your boss was a vegetarian.'

2 **Rewrite the sentences so that they have the same meaning, using *could have*.**

1 Perhaps Kate's forgotten that we invited her.
Kate could have forgotten that we invited her.
2 It's possible that Elena ate your sandwich.
Elena ____________
3 Maybe you left your wallet in the bank.
You ____________
4 Jason may have caught an earlier train.
Jason ____________
5 Maybe they went to the wrong place to meet us.
They ____________
6 It's possible that I was out when you called.
I ____________
7 Dave might have got stuck in traffic.
Dave ____________
8 Perhaps you left the caps lock key on.
You ____________

3 **What would you say in these situations? Complete the sentences with *should(n't) have*, and the verbs in brackets.**

1 You left your car in a car park without buying a ticket. You have to pay a €50 fine.
I *should have bought a ticket* (buy)
2 You told your best friend Anna a secret. She told your boyfriend Tom.
You ____________ (tell)
3 You've been waiting one hour for a bus because you thought a taxi was too expensive.
We ____________ (take)
4 Your colleague has made a decision without discussing something with you first.
You ____________ (discuss)
5 Your friend's laptop was stolen from his car.
He ____________ (leave)
6 You cooked steak for a dinner party, but nobody told you that Gerard was a vegetarian.
Someone ____________ (tell)
7 You stayed out really late last night, and now you're late for work.
I ____________ (stay)
8 Your friend didn't study for an exam, and he failed.
He ____________

4 **Imagine you are alive 100 years ago. Make sentences about your life, using *would(n't)* have.**

1 *I wouldn't have had a computer.*
2 ______________________
3 ______________________
4 ______________________
5 ______________________
6 ______________________
7 ______________________
8 ______________________

5 **Correct the mistake in each sentence below.**

1 Why didn't you tell me about her problem?
have said
I wouldn't ^say what I did.
2 You shouldn't taken her book without asking first.
3 They still haven't confirmed delivery. We could have sent it to the wrong address?
4 Rio really shouldn't have gived up football. He was so talented.
5 I wouldn't have stop to break up the fight like Mike did. It was too dangerous.
6 Fatih and Vera could have known about the party, or they would have come.
7 I know I should have to call you sooner, but I've been so busy.
8 Thanks for all your help, I could have done it without you.
9 In your position, I would backed up my files first.
10 The doctor should have tell you sooner.

6 **Complete the sentences with a phrase from the box and the correct form of the verb in brackets.**

could have (x2)	couldn't have	should have (x2)	shouldn't have
would have (x2)	wouldn't have		

1 Oh no, I've forgotten Marcel's address. I knew I *should have written* (write) it down.
2 Why didn't you buy them that picture? I'm sure they ______________ (like) it.
3 We did our best to catch the train: we ______________ (run) any faster.
4 You ______________ (listen) to Paul. You know he has some stupid ideas.
5 The room was a terrible mess when the men had finished painting it. I ______________ (do) it myself.
6 Look where you're going – we were really close to that car. We ______________ (have) an accident.
7 You were right not to tell her the truth about Brian: she ______________ (believe) you, anyway.
8 Rupert ______________ (be) a great pianist, but he didn't practise enough.
9 I like Kristin's new motorbike, but I ______________ (buy) a bigger one.

Pronunciation

Past modal forms in connected speech

7a 🎧 **12.1 Listen to these sentences and choose the phrase you hear.**

1 You ***should read*** / ***should have read*** the instructions first.
2 We ***could walk*** / ***could have walked*** to the party.
3 The hotel doesn't look very nice in the photos. I ***wouldn't stay*** / ***wouldn't have stayed*** there.
4 You ***could invite*** / ***could have invited*** Sarah to your party.
5 I think we're lost. We ***shouldn't turn*** / ***shouldn't have turned*** left at the traffic lights.
6 That computer was so cheap. Why didn't you buy it? ***I'd buy*** / ***I would have bought*** two!

b Listen again. Practise saying the sentences.

Language focus 2

Imaginary situations in the past with *if*

8 Match the sentence beginnings in A with the endings in B.

A

1 If I hadn't forgotten my passport [c]
2 If Sara and I had stayed longer in Paris [ ]
3 If we'd booked our theatre tickets in advance [ ]
4 If Greta hadn't bought a new coat [ ]
5 If Malcolm had studied more [ ]
6 If my uncle lived near the airport [ ]
7 If it hadn't rained [ ]
8 If you hadn't taken so long to get ready [ ]

B

a she'd have enough money to pay her rent.
b I'd have stayed at his house on my way to Germany.
c I'd be on the plane to Tunisia.
d we wouldn't have had to queue outside.
e we could have taken the children to the zoo.
f we wouldn't have missed our bus.
g he wouldn't have failed his exam.
h we'd have gone up the Eiffel Tower.

9 Circle the correct option in each sentence.

1 If Marcelo ***hadn't worked*** / ***didn't work*** so hard when he was younger, he wouldn't be so successful now.
2 Jitesh and Maria ***wouldn't have been*** / ***wouldn't be*** getting divorced now if they'd tried a bit harder in the past.
3 If you'd left a bit earlier, you would ***arrive*** / ***have arrived*** on time.
4 We could ***pick you up*** / ***have picked you up*** on the way here if we'd known you were coming.
5 What would you be doing now if you ***hadn't*** / ***didn't*** become a teacher?
6 If we ***hadn't missed*** / ***didn't miss*** the plane we would be lying on the beach right now!
7 If the referee hadn't disallowed that goal, ***we would have won*** / ***would win*** the game last night.
8 The film would have been more successful if they ***had cast*** / ***cast*** more famous actors.
9 If you ***didn't walk*** / ***hadn't walked*** into the café at that moment, we would never have met.
10 Where would you ***be*** / ***have been*** now if you hadn't moved here?

10a Read the following newspaper article and answer the questions.

1 Why did Prasad run away from home?

______

______

______

2 What did his family think had happened to him?

______

______

______

A BRIGHT SPARK

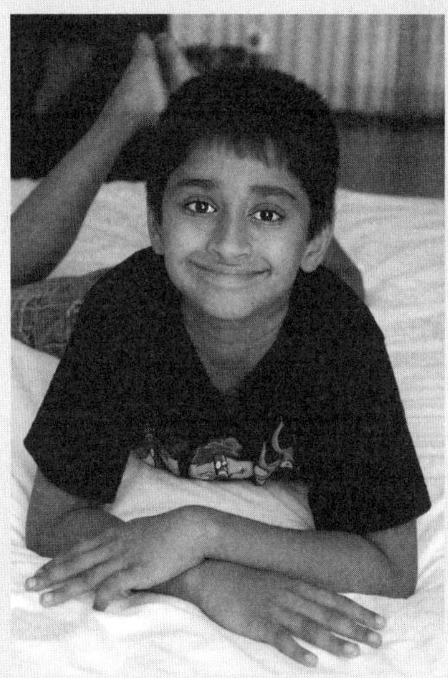

The family of an Indian boy who disappeared from home two years ago were amazed to see him on TV receiving a national award.

Prasad Akkonan's relatives had started to think the boy must be dead when they saw him winning the award for being top scorer in his exam.

Prasad ran away from home 'to become something in life' after his family forced him to enrol in an electrician's course against his wishes.

He went to Bombay and then to Nangpur where he worked as a waiter at a tea stall during the day, and studied at night. His family had no idea what had happened to him until they saw him receiving his award for scoring 86.5 percent, the highest amongst millions of students in his Higher Secondary Exam.

b Use the prompts to make sentences about the story.

1 If / he / not / decide / 'become something in life' / he / not / run away.

If he hadn't decided to 'become something in life', he wouldn't have run away.

2 If / he / not / run away / he / do / an electrician's course.

______

3 If / he / stay / at home / he / be / an electrician now.

______

4 He / not / have / enough money to study / if / he / not / work / as a waiter.

______

5 If / he / write / to his parents / they / not / think / he was dead.

______

6 If / they / not / see / the programme / they / still / think / he was dead.

______

7 He / not / have / score / 86.5 percent / if / he / not / work hard.

______

8 If / he / not / be / very clever / he / not / won / the award.

______

Vocabulary

Problems and solutions

11 Match sentences 1–8 with the endings a–h.

1 When he started getting headaches after reading, [c]
2 We need to make a decision. [ ]
3 I wish I had someone sympathetic [ ]
4 You can try and ignore the problem all you want, [ ]
5 Abi decided to trust her intuition and [ ]
6 Tom is the calmest person I know. [ ]
7 Astrid was losing sleep over her problem, [ ]
8 I'm sick of this. We need to work together and [ ]

a but it won't go away by itself.
b so she decided to talk it over with her mother.
c Marco realised he had a problem with his eyes.
d sort it out once and for all.
e who understood my concerns.
f Do you want to go out or stay in tonight?
g tell Paul the relationship was over.
h It's almost as if he doesn't have a care in the world.

Listen and read

The greatest romantic films of all time

12a 12.2 Listen and read about three films and match each with its title.

1 *Doctor Zhivago* ______
2 *Casablanca* ______
3 *Titanic* ______

b Listen and read again and answer the questions.

1 Where does each film take place?
a ______
b ______
c ______
2 Each film is about three people. Who are they?
a ______
b ______
c ______
3 Is the ending happy or sad or both?
a ______
b ______
c ______

A
One of the most beloved of American films, this is a classic story of a love triangle between two men and one woman. It is the story of Rick Blaine (Humphrey Bogart) who runs a nightclub in a town in Morocco during World War II. Rick's café has become a place where people can get illegal papers to help them to escape from Europe to the USA. One day, to Rick's horror, Ilsa (Ingrid Bergman) walks through the door of his café ('Of all the gin joints in all the towns in all the world, she walks into mine'). Rick and Ilsa were lovers in Paris before the war but he thinks that she left him. Their romantic feelings soon return but Rick and Ilsa must face a painful choice: should Ilsa go to the USA with her husband, Victor (an important war hero who needs her support) or should she stay with Rick, the love of her life? In the end Bogart makes the decision for her and does the hardest thing for any man in love. He lets her go, in one of the most famous goodbye scenes ever recorded on film, as he wipes away her tears and says: 'Here's looking at you kid.'

B
The romance in this film is tragic because it is so intense and lasts for such a short time. And because it is only a small part of a terrible and huge drama. A voyage on a ship going to New York brings together Rose, a high-class 17-year-old girl, and a third-class passenger. Everyone who has seen this movie remembers Kate Winslet and Leonardo Di Caprio together at the bow of the ship, the wind blowing in their hair and their hearts full of hope ('Jack, I'm flying!'). She thinks her biggest problem is to decide whether to marry her rich fiancé or to leave him for her new love. We know that in the next three hours they will both face terrible danger and that he will have to die so that she can live.

C
The music is unforgettable, the photography is extraordinary and the romance is moving. Against the background of the Russian Revolution, this is the story of a doctor who is in love with two women, one of them his wife and the other his lover (Lara). Omar Sharif and Julie Christie play the lovers who are separated and then brought back together again by war and destiny. Everyone suffers in this powerful but tiny human story and also in the bigger story of the events of the Revolution. The film is about the choices people have to make between love and duty to their family and to their country. Eventually, Lara and the doctor decide to part but the ending is not completely sad. Many years later we see that their daughter has survived and the future for her looks more hopeful.

Writing

A letter to sort out a problem

13a Lucy is talking to her friend Anya about a problem. Complete her conversation with the words in the box.

~~booked~~ received booking sent dates
paid write heard

A: Hi Lucy, how are things with you?
L: Oh, hi Anya, good to see you. To be honest I'm a bit worried at the moment.
A: Why's that?
L: Well I [1] *booked* a flight to Mexico City on the internet the other week, it was just the kind of thing I was looking for. I [2]__________ by credit card and [3]__________ the tickets a few days later.
A: So what was the problem?
L: When I looked at the tickets, the [4]__________ were wrong! I checked my [5]__________ and the travel agent had made a mistake.
A: Oh no! Did you contact them?
L: Yes, of course. I [6]__________ the tickets straight back, but that was nearly two weeks ago and I haven't [7]__________ anything back yet.
A: Well I think you should [8]__________ to them. They might pay more attention if it's written down.
L: OK, thanks Anya. I'll do that then.

b Lucy has written a letter to sort out the problem. Read the letter and put the sentences a–h in the correct order.

44 Barn Road
Nottingham, NS4

29th May
The Manager Eurotrips Travel Agents

Dear Sir / Madam,

a A week later, I received my credit card receipt and the ticket, but unfortunately the dates were wrong.

b That was ten days ago, and I've heard nothing from you since.

c You booked me onto a flight costing €975, which I paid for by credit card.

d I look forward to hearing from you.

e As you can imagine, I am very concerned about this because I need to make other arrangements for my trip, which I cannot do until the dates are confirmed.

f Several weeks ago I telephoned your office to book a return flight to Mexico City, leaving on 8th July and returning 27th July.

g I would therefore be grateful if you would look into this matter urgently.

h I immediately returned the ticket by registered post, with a note explaining the problem.

Yours faithfully,
L Humphries

c Write a letter to sort out the problem below. Show your letter to your teacher.

Three weeks ago, you booked a four-week course at the Best Language School, 354 Liffey Road, Dublin DN6. A week ago, you had not received a receipt or confirmation of your place on the course. You phoned the school and left a message on the answering machine, but you have still not heard anything.

Before you write the letter, decide:

- how many hours a day your course is.
- how you paid for the course (credit card / bank transfer).
- the dates of your course.

Audio script

UNIT 1 RECORDING 1

1 A: Do you like our new teacher? B: Yes, I do.
2 A: Have you got the time? B: No, I haven't.
3 A: Is it cold outside today? B: No, it isn't.
4 A: Did you have a good holiday? B: Yes, I did.
5 A: Was there a lot of traffic on the roads this morning? B: Yes, there was.
6 A: Are your neighbours nice? B: Yes, they are.
7 A: Were you at the football match on Saturday? B: Yes, I was.
8 A: Has your brother got a girlfriend? B: No, he hasn't.
9 A: Does it take long to do this exercise? B: No, it doesn't.
10 A: Was the film good? B: No, it wasn't.

UNIT 1 RECORDING 2

1 Where exactly do you live?
2 How do you spell your name?
3 Have you got any brothers and sisters?
4 No, I haven't.
5 Which one would you like?
6 Does your mother speak English?
7 Yes, actually she does.
8 How was your weekend?
9 What's your date of birth?
10 What time do you usually get up in the morning?

UNIT 1 RECORDING 3

Charlotte from Bristol

My 'hero' at the moment is Ricky. We work together. I was thinking of leaving the place where I work because of our horrible new boss. He's always in a bad mood and he never has a good word to say to anyone. He also picks on young female members of staff. There's a girl called Kimberley who's terrified of him. Or at least she was. When Ricky joined us, everything changed.

First he covered for me when I was late back from lunch by telling the boss that I was downstairs in the photocopying room. Then, a couple of days later, the boss was standing at Kimberley's desk, shouting at her, telling her she was lazy and would have to stay late to finish her work ... Anyway, Ricky marched straight up to him and told him he was a pathetic coward for talking to his staff like that. Well, the boss was stunned to silence – he just walked off without saying another word and he's left us alone since then.

Dan from Newcastle

I'm writing to tell you about my niece, Mary. She's only seven and she's in hospital at the moment. She was in a bad car accident two weeks ago and she broke both her legs. She's had one operation and now she's waiting for another, then she'll have to be in a wheelchair for quite a while. Anyway, I am constantly amazed by this little girl's courage. She never cries when she has an injection, and very rarely complains about the considerable pain that she must be in. When I go in to visit her she always has a smile for me, and last time I went she was comforting another girl who was upset because her parents couldn't come and visit her. I've also noticed that she shares all the chocolates and toys that people have given her with the other children in her ward. I don't know how many adults would be as generous as that!

Annette from Leeds

I'm hoping that by writing to you, I might be able to get in touch with my 'hero' again. I don't know him – I don't even know his name – but what he did was unbelievably kind and honest. I went shopping at my local supermarket last Friday, and I met an old friend at the checkout desk. We chatted for a while, then I loaded up the car and came home. It was only then that I realised I'd lost my purse: I thought maybe I'd dropped it in the car park. I started to panic when I also remembered that I had quite a lot of money in it. Then someone knocked at the door and it was a complete stranger, holding out my purse! He said he was in the queue behind me at the supermarket checkout and that's where he found my purse. He got my address from my driving licence. I was so grateful, but I didn't know what to say. Anyway, he just walked off, and I haven't been able to thank him properly.

UNIT 1 RECORDING 4

1 A: I'm working in advertising at the moment.
B: Are you? That sounds interesting.
2 A: I don't get on very well with my brother.
B: Don't you? Why's that then?
3 A: I've never seen the sea.
B: Haven't you? That's amazing!
4 A: We once shared a flat together.
B: Did you? When was that?
5 A: I'm thinking of going to Spain this year.
B: Are you? Where exactly?
6 A: Our class was really interesting today.
B: Was it? What did you do?
7 A: Annika went skiing last month.
B: Did she? That sounds fun!
8 A: Dave and I both have the same surname.
B: Do you? What a coincidence!

UNIT 2 RECORDING 1

1 It happened a long time ago.
2 We stopped for lunch.
3 He travelled a long way.
4 It looked strange.
5 She reminded me to lock the car.
6 We visited some old friends.
7 I phoned you this morning.
8 He changed his name.
9 We practised our song.
10 They opened their presents.
11 The weather improved and we went out.
12 We received a lot of emails.
13 They repeated the news at ten o'clock.
14 I answered all the questions.

UNIT 2 RECORDING 2

1 I used to believe that countries really had their names written across them and that when you reached a border there would be red dotted lines on the ground.
2 I used to think that the trails that aeroplanes leave across the sky are created by the pilots leaning out of the windows holding a piece of chalk, so they know where they've been. That's what I was told, anyway.
3 I used to have problems when I was trying to learn how to read a real clock. My theory was that if an hour is longer than a minute, then the long hand was the hour and the short hand was for minutes. I was always late coming home ... or really early.
4 I remember I used to be very scared of swallowing seeds when I was small. Once when I swallowed a lemon pip, I refused to open my mouth in the morning because I thought that the branches of the lemon tree that had grown in the night would come out.
5 When I was about six or seven years old, I used to believe that a little penguin lived in my refrigerator and his job was to turn the interior light on and off. I used to sit and open the fridge repeatedly, trying to catch him doing it.
6 For some reason, I used to think that there was a big red button in the middle of the president's desk, and if he pressed it the whole world would explode. I also thought that it wasn't very well guarded, and I always worried that he would accidentally lean on it.
7 One time when I was about to pour a drink from a bottle of diet coke, my sister said 'You know, diet coke turns you into a skeleton if you're not fat.' I was terrified. Unfortunately for me, her lie worked and I didn't drink any diet drinks until I was in my teens.
8 When I was a child, I couldn't understand how a radio made in Japan could play songs in Spanish and English. If they are made in Japan, they should just be able to play Japanese songs.
9 During my first few years at school, I kept hearing that 'teachers have eyes in the back of their heads' so I thought that when someone became a teacher, they had to have an operation to get an extra set of eyes! I also wondered why a lot of lady teachers had long hair. What's the point of having eyes in the back of your head if you keep covering them up?

10 I used to believe (and still do actually!) that animals could watch TV and understand what they were seeing. I had a rabbit that just sat near the screen, staring at it while the show was on, but would look away or do something else when the ads came on. Now my two dogs act in the same way – they sit with me and watch TV, but then start to yawn and stretch during the ads – except dog food commercials, of course!

UNIT 2 RECORDING 3

1 When you argue with a friend, do you forget about it quickly and stay friends?
2 Do you find it easy to remember people's names?
3 When did you last forget someone's birthday?
4 Is it easy to recognise your handwriting?
5 Do you remind people of anyone in your family?
6 How often do you forget your keys?
7 Can you remember your first day at school?
8 Do you usually recognise famous people when you see them on TV?
9 Do you remember meeting your best friend for the first time?
10 What sort of things do people have to remind you to do?

UNIT 2 RECORDING 4

I was getting dressed when Guy phoned and said he was ill, so I decided to go by train. Unfortunately, while I was talking to Guy on the phone, the cat walked over my shirt so I had to iron another one. When I was walking to the station, it started snowing and I got cold. The train was delayed because it started snowing and when it finally arrived, I was frozen. I fell asleep while I was sitting on the train and missed my station. I got off at the next station and decided to walk to Kyra's house. When I reached the end of the road I realised I was lost. I didn't have my mobile so I looked for a phone box to call a taxi. When I arrived at Kyra's house, it was nearly midnight and people were going home!

UNIT 3 RECORDING 1

Unusual holidays

The Legendary Ghan Opal Safari

This is an extraordinary five-day journey from Adelaide on the south coast to Alice Springs, with an overnight tour to Coober Pedy, where 70 percent of the world's opals are mined. The Ghan is one of Australia's most luxurious trains: you will be travelling across a hostile landscape of desert, salt lakes, mountains and hot springs, but in true comfort whether you travel first class or not. At Coober Pedy, the temperatures are so extreme (up to 50°C during the day and 0°C at night) that all the houses are built underground as well as the mines. You stay at the Desert Cave Hotel, where the rooms have been cut out of the rock.

Tours are throughout the year and cost $952.

The Final Frontier: 3,400 kph

Journey to the edge of space in a Russian Foxbat jetfighter. Arrive in Moscow and spend a day training and preparing for the flight. Then travel at more than twice the speed of sound, to over 24,000 metres above the Earth. Join those few free spirits that have already experienced this journey to the edge of space. At about 32 kilometres above the ground, the curvature of the earth comes dramatically into view. In the cockpit of a Russian MiG-25 military fighter plane, you're aboard the fastest combat aircraft in the world.

Limited dates. Contact us direct for details and cost.

Wilderness Husky Adventure

Head up to Lapland and experience the thrill of a husky sledging expedition. Drive your own team of huskies and stay overnight in a traditional wooden lodge, where you can relax and enjoy a traditional sauna. Drive a snowmobile, and with luck see the famous northern lights (aurora borealis), a wonderful natural display of green, red and purple lights in the sky.

Finish your trip by staying in the Icehotel – a hotel made completely of ice! This is a really unforgettable and unique short break.

December to April. Three nights for $2,300.

Storm Chasing

Witness spectacular explosive thunderstorms, lightning and tornadoes. Come with us as we follow the storm and get as close as we can, to give you the most exciting experience. Our vans are equipped with the latest storm-chasing technology, like our Weather Radar System, In-Motion Satellite Tracking System, and Lightning Display System that shows storms and lightning up to 500 kilometres away. We travel as far as necessary to see the tornadoes: the chase could take you anywhere in Texas, Oklahoma, Kansas or Eastern Colorado.

May and June only.

Six days for $2,400.

Luxury Under Water

Jules' Undersea Lodge in Key Largo, Florida was originally built as La Chalupa mobile undersea laboratory, the largest and most technically advanced in the world. The Lodge has been completely remodelled to provide guests with luxury living space for up to six people. The interior has two living chambers, with bedrooms and dining and entertainment facilities.

Earn an Aquanaut certificate while enjoying unlimited diving for certified divers, a gourmet dinner prepared by a 'mer-chef', and a gourmet breakfast. If desired, guests may spend several days underwater without surfacing. You can even have your underwater wedding here.

All year round. From $325 per night.

White Shark Heaven, Mexico

The world's ultimate shark dive and fishing adventure is closer than you think. For divers, non-divers and tuna fishermen, discover Isla Guadalupe, one of the world's most exciting new Great White dive sites. Your cage dive and world-class tuna-fishing expedition takes you on a five-day live-aboard adventure to the newly discovered and beautiful Isla Guadalupe site off the coast of Mexico. You will have the opportunity to dive by day with Great White Sharks and fish for huge tuna in the hunting grounds of Great Whites and Mako sharks.

Seven-Day Live-Aboard Expeditions: October to November from $2,380.

UNIT 3 RECORDING 2

1 My city is a lot bigger than it was 20 years ago.
2 Peru is the third largest country in South America.
3 Australian English is similar to British English.
4 The shops here are not as good as in my country.
5 There were fewer cars here in the past.
6 My language is very different from English.

UNIT 3 RECORDING 3

1 Do you know when the next bus goes to Central Park?
2 Could you tell me what time the train arrives?
3 Do you know how much it will cost?
4 Do you know where I have to change?
5 Could you tell me which platform the train to Paris goes from?
6 Do you know which bus this is?
7 Do you know when the next one is?
8 Could you tell me how I get to the airport?

UNIT 4 RECORDING 1

It was my birthday yesterday: I'm 14 years old. Some people say I'm lucky but I don't think so. Imagine, in my life I've been to eight different schools and I've never stayed anywhere long enough to make a best friend. We've lived in so many different houses that I can't remember some of them. In fact, last year we moved house three times. It's true, there are some good things. I've met some really famous people and we've had some great holidays – I've been to Disneyland at least four times, but never with mum and dad. When I was young, I always had a nanny, and she took me on holiday. I'm staying with my aunt and uncle at the moment because my dad's making a film in France and my mum's gone to Los Angeles.

Audio script

UNIT 4 RECORDING 2

1 The film started ten minutes ago.
2 Did Stefano come to class yesterday?
3 I've done all the exercises in this unit so far.
4 She's only seen her brother twice in the last ten years.
5 I started learning English in 2010.
6 He's lived here since 2005.
7 What was your favourite game when you were young?

UNIT 4 RECORDING 3

1 I've been looking for a flat for about a month.
2 They've played ten games since August.
3 She's only been here for a couple of minutes.
4 I've been writing this report since 11 o'clock.
5 I've been living in Canada since I was eight.
6 He went to Brazil a couple of months ago.

UNIT 4 RECORDING 4

Johnny Depp Born: **June 9, 1963**

Where: **Owensboro, Kentucky**

Rare among American actors, Depp has made a name for himself, effortlessly switching between mainstream Hollywood movies and more 'out of the ordinary' projects. Talking about his choice of roles, he once said: 'With any part you play, there is a certain amount of yourself in it. There has to be, otherwise it's not acting. It's lying.' Highlights of a richly diverse career include *Edward Scissorhands*, *Sleepy Hollow* and *Pirates of the Caribbean*.

Depp dropped out of school at 16 to concentrate on a career in music, playing the guitar (he played with more than 20 bands). However, his musical career failed to take off, and he found himself selling pens over the phone to pay the bills. His lucky break came when make-up artist Lori Allison, to whom he was briefly married, introduced him to Nicolas Cage. Although at first they did not like each other, they later became good friends and Cage persuaded him to try acting. Depp signed on with Cage's agent, and made his feature film debut in Wes Craven's horror film *Nightmare on Elm Street*, in which the character he played was eaten by his bed. After that, he had his first screen leading role in *Private Resort*.

Depp went on to achieve teen idol status in the TV series *21 Jump Street*, but after four seasons, he wanted out, with the hope of making the transition to the big screen. He starred in *Cry-Baby*, followed by Tim Burton's *Edward Scissorhands*, after which he went on to win considerable critical acclaim in *Ed Wood*, a reunion with Burton. Depp made his feature directorial debut with *The Brave* in 1997, a film he also co-wrote and starred in. Premiering at the Cannes Film Festival, the film also featured Marlon Brando, but earned mostly negative reviews, with most critics blaming its weak script. *Sleepy Hollow* teamed him with director Burton yet again, before he starred in Ted Demme's *Blow*, and appeared in the thriller *From Hell*, about Jack the Ripper.

Off screen, his good looks and 'bad boy' image (he was once arrested for attacking intrusive paparazzi with a wooden plank) have earned him a lot of media attention. He was voted one of the 50 most beautiful people in the world by *People* magazine in 1996. He has also had his fair share of celebrity romances. When his engagement to *Edward Scissorhands* co-star Winona Ryder ended, he had a tattoo (one of about 13), which said 'Winona Forever', altered by laser to get rid of the last two letters of her name. His relationship with model Kate Moss also ended abruptly in 1998, when he started dating French singer-actress Vanessa Paradis. They now have two children, Lily-Rose Melody and Jack.

More recent work has included *Pirates of the Caribbean* with Geoffrey Rush, *Once Upon A Time In Mexico*, *Alice in Wonderland* and *Dark Shadows*.

UNIT 5 RECORDING 1

1	succeed	7	failure
2	experience	8	imagine
3	productive	9	experienced
4	profitable	10	improvement
5	distraction	11	knowledgeable
6	imagination	12	know

UNIT 5 RECORDING 2

Gemma

I absolutely love music and listen to it all the time, even when I go jogging. Of course I have to look after my voice. I do exercises for three hours every day and I take lots of vitamin C. If I get a sore throat, I go straight to bed and rest. I usually try to get at least eight hours sleep a night anyway. ... As for my job – you really can't be shy in this kind of work, and you have to be very patient because sometimes we practise for hours before we get it right. When we're on tour, we work for several weeks with no breaks and you can get really tired. For relaxation, whenever I get a holiday, I go straight to a sunny beach, but the thing I enjoy the most is the great feeling you get from a live audience.

Raoul

Well, my work's really quite stressful. Most people think you spend your day chopping vegetables and stirring soup, but it's not that simple. You have to be really careful with the food and keep everything very clean. The big problem is my boss – he shouts at me all the time – even, for example, if I forget to wash up one plate – I just can't do anything right sometimes. Actually, I'm hoping to find a new job soon because I don't get much time off. I'd like to have more weekends free, to see friends and to spend more time with my two little boys. You know, it's strange spending all day with food – when I go home I just want to eat a sandwich or a bag of chips and I'm terribly critical when I eat in a restaurant.

Frank

Well, I first got interested because I loved doing them so much myself – I used to do at least one every day. I suppose I've got the right kind of mind really – I enjoy playing around with puzzles, especially word puzzles. So I sent a couple in to a local newspaper and was really surprised when they asked me for more. I suppose it is a strange way to spend your day – surrounded by dictionaries and books, but it's great that I can organise my own time, so I try to finish by two and then I can take my dog for a walk. It's very satisfying though – I love the feeling after I've thought of the final clue, and it all fits together. It's also really nice when people write to me and thank me.

Funny really, because I'm just doing what I like.

Megan

People sometimes ask me if I forget which country I'm in or what time of day it is, but I guess I've got used to it. Last week I was in London and tomorrow I'm going to Hong Kong. I'm based in Bahrain, and I have a small apartment there, although I sometimes don't spend more than seven or eight days a month there. The thing I like most about my job is the contact with the people from different cultures. The idea that it's a glamorous job is a bit of a cliché – you spend a lot of your time handing out food and drinks and clearing up people's rubbish. I certainly don't feel very glamorous at two in the morning! Actually, there are a lot of things that we're trained to do that people don't realise – like fight fires, deliver babies, survive in the desert or ocean.

UNIT 5 RECORDING 3

A: Good afternoon, Henderson Insurance, Pam speaking. How can I help?
B: Good afternoon, I'd like to speak to Mrs Leeson, please.
A: Just a moment, I'll put you through.
C: Hello, Mrs Leeson's office, Sandy speaking.
B: Hello, could I speak to Mrs Leeson, please?
C: I'll just see if she's available. Can I ask who's calling?
B: Jo Spinelli.
C: One moment, please. Hello, I'm afraid she's not in the office at the moment.
B: OK, could you ask her to call me back?
C: Certainly. Could I take your number?
B: Yes, it's 4442 123 451.
C: Right, I'll get her to call you back as soon as she comes in.
B: Thank you. Goodbye.
C: Goodbye.

UNIT 6 RECORDING 1

1 She'd remembered to call her mum.
2 I found the one I was looking for.
3 I'd heard you were in town.
4 John had left the book in the car.
5 We thought about staying at home.
6 I'd booked the table for six o'clock.
7 He emailed me last week.
8 We'd met in a restaurant.

UNIT 6 RECORDING 2

He told me his name was Sam Boyd, but I found out later that his real name is Michael Rackham.

He said he lived in Los Angeles and that he was an actor but actually he had never had a job or a permanent address. The worst thing was that he said he wasn't seeing anyone and that he had never been married, but the police records showed that he already has three 'wives'; one in Texas, one in Turkey and one in Austria. And as for the woman in Florida, he said that he had been engaged to; we found out later that he was talking about his sister who lives there! He told me he would be in the UK on business in March. He'll get an unwelcome surprise then. The police will be waiting for him!

UNIT 6 RECORDING 3

1 Where are you from?
2 Are you here on holiday?
3 Are you travelling alone?
4 Did you pack your suitcases yourself?
5 Have you been to the USA before?
6 How long will you be in the country?
7 Do you know anyone in San Francisco?
8 Where are you going to stay?
9 How much money do you have with you?

UNIT 6 RECORDING 4

The top joke in the UK

A woman gets on a bus with her baby. The bus driver says, 'That's the ugliest baby I've ever seen!' The woman is furious. She says to a man sitting next to her, 'The driver was extremely rude to me.' The man says, 'Go and speak to him. Go ahead, I'll hold your monkey for you.'

The top joke in Northern Ireland

A doctor says to his patient, 'I have bad news and worse news.' 'Oh dear, what's the bad news?' asks the patient. The doctor replies, 'You only have 24 hours to live.' 'That's terrible,' says the patient. 'How can the news possibly be worse?' The doctor replies, 'I've been trying to contact you since yesterday.'

The top joke in Canada

When the space organisation NASA first started sending up astronauts they discovered ballpoint pens would not work in zero gravity. To solve the problem, NASA scientists spent ten years and $12 billion to develop a pen that would write in zero gravity, upside down, under water, on all types of surface, and at temperatures ranging from below freezing to 300°C. The Russians used a pencil.

The top joke in Germany

A general noticed one of his soldiers behaving strangely. The soldier used to pick up every piece of paper that he saw, look at it, and say, 'That's not it.' This went on for some time until the general arranged for a psychologist to see the man. The psychologist decided that the man was crazy and wrote a letter to say he should leave the army. The soldier picked it up, smiled and said, 'That's it!'

The top joke in the world

Two New Jersey hunters are out in the woods when one of them falls down. He doesn't seem to be breathing and he looks very white. The other man takes out his phone and calls the emergency services. 'My friend is dead! What can I do?' The operator says, 'Calm down. I can help. First go and make sure he is dead.' There is a silence, then a shot is heard. Back on the phone, the man says, 'OK, what next?'

UNIT 7 RECORDING 1

A Well done Channel 10 for the brilliant series *City Mysteries*. The acting was amazing and the stories didn't try too hard – genuinely interesting without trying to be too shocking. I was so disappointed when it finished. Are there plans for a new series?

B I'm rather confused about ABC's policy on not showing violence before 9 pm. I watched *The Precinct* at 8.30 p.m. last Thursday and was shocked at the amount of violence shown. I must say I'm quite annoyed with ABC for making my ten-year-old daughter sit through this.

C I was really pleased when I saw that *Celebrity Spot* was back on SBS. I always look forward to the programme because it has such inspiring guests. However, last Friday's show was very disappointing – the interviewer asked such stupid questions and hardly gave Rihanna a chance to speak!

UNIT 7 RECORDING 2

1 A: I bet Tessa was happy about her exam results.
B: Oh yes, she was absolutely delighted.
2 A: I'm not going in – the water's freezing!
B: Oh come on, it's not that cold.
3 A: You're not frightened of spiders, are you?
B: Oh yes I am – absolutely terrified, in fact.
4 A: Have you seen the ridiculous outfit that Roberta's wearing?
B: Oh yes, she does look a bit silly, doesn't she?
5 A: I thought there were some really hilarious moments in that film.
B: Did you? I didn't think it was that funny.
6 A: And now to the sad news about Ernie Hope.
B: Yes, his death will be a tragic loss for the entertainment industry.
7 A: I was astonished when Will told me about his divorce.
B: I know, it was a surprise, wasn't it?
8 A: You look hot – do you want a cold drink?
B: Yes, please, it's absolutely boiling outside.

UNIT 7 RECORDING 3

1	terrified	excellent
2	astonished	awful
3	boiling	furious
4	exhausted	delighted
5	excellent	hilarious
6	awful	freezing
7	hilarious	ridiculous
8	terrible	furious

UNIT 7 RECORDING 4

1

More of the King's top tunes and a follow up to last year's smash hit album *Elvis Number Ones*, released at a time when the King's popularity is at an all time high. Two tracks stand out from the norm: a curious remix of *Rubberneckin'*, and an unreleased version of *I'm a Routabout*. Both songs are enjoyable to listen to, but not strong enough to be hits.

The rest of the album sounds like many an Elvis compilation of the last two and a half decades, with plenty of old classics and fans' favourites. Some of the highlights which non-fans as well as fans may enjoy are: *Loving You*, *I Need Your Love Tonight*, *Bossa Nova Baby* (potential remix material here?), *Always On My Mind* and *Moody Blue*. *Moody Blue* is a very good song, although recorded at a time when Elvis was not in great health. I believe this could have been a big smash hit for Elvis if it had come along in 1970–73 when he may have had more energy to put into the song, rather than 1976–77.

If you don't already have a lot of the songs on this CD then this is for you, especially as the technical sound quality of the songs will be better than on previous releases.

Audio script

2

This movie is far too short when you compare it to its predecessors, but in its 109 minutes you get more action than the first two movies combined, and you also get a great story.

The effects are second to none, which you expect with a Terminator movie and the pace starts at a blinding speed and never slows. There are some great moments of continuity from the first two movies and one or two cameos and returns of past characters. The movie is also not afraid to have its funny moments, such as Arnie walking into a nightclub naked on ladies' night in search of clothing. The scene also gives some light relief from the movie's otherwise somewhat negative feel as humanity rolls closer to impending disaster.

While I may sound a little unpopular, I rate this instalment higher than its predecessors: the director does a better job than Cameron could ever hope to do. This is a fantastic chase movie, even more so than T2 ever was, and with T4 already written, I am eager to see what will happen next in the saga. And no, I didn't miss Linda Hamilton as much as I thought I would: this movie has proved that it can do just as well, if not better, without her presence.

3

Until this summer, I have been guilty of writing off the Harry Potter books as 'mere children's books'. But after finally taking the time to read them, I realised what I have been missing all this time. Sure, they are kid-friendly, but they are witty, clever and can be enjoyed by even a college student like myself. And I am very pleased to say that they get better and better with each installment. *Order of the Phoenix* takes a distinctly dark tone that was hinted at in *Goblet of Fire*. Harry is not a young kid any more, and yes, he is angry a lot, but with everything that he has had to deal with, he has every right to be. There is, of course, Voldemort on the loose and the Ministry of Magic trying to cover it up (a source of political satire in this novel). There is also a much-hyped 'death of a central character'. I won't reveal who the unfortunate person is, but I was quite upset when Rowling killed him / her off. That is yet another testament to her genius, the fact that she makes you care so much about her characters.

I thoroughly enjoyed this book. Anyone with a sense of fun and imagination should. It may not be a literary masterpiece, but it doesn't need to be. It's just fun. And yes, it's long, but it moves so fast that you can hardly believe that there are nearly 800 pages!

UNIT 7 RECORDING 5

1 A: I'm phoning to ask if you'd like to come over for dinner.
B: That sounds great. What time shall I come?
2 A: I've got two tickets for *Rejection* at the cinema on Saturday. Would you like to come?
B: I'm sorry I can't. It's my sister's birthday.
3 A: Great. Can you give me a ring when you get there?
B: OK, will do.
4 A: Are you free later? Do you want to go for some food?
B: Yeah, I'd love to!
5 A: What about meeting at Phil's flat first?
B: OK, I'll see you there.
6 A: Are you free this evening?
B: No, sorry ... I'm having dinner with Cheryl.

UNIT 8 RECORDING 1

1 A: Is it all right if I close the window?
B: Yes, go ahead.
2 A: Would you mind helping me with my suitcase?
B: I'm sorry but I've got a bad back.
3 A: Could you pass the salt, please?
B: Yes, here you are.
4 A: Would you bring us the bill, please?
B: Certainly, sir.
5 A: Do you mind if I go now?
B: No, that's fine. I think we've finished.
6 A: Would you mind getting me some milk?
B: Of course not. How much do you need?
7 A: Could I possibly have a look at your newspaper?
B: Of course.
8 A: Would you mind answering my phone while I'm out?
B: I'm afraid I can't. I'm just going to a meeting.

UNIT 8 RECORDING 2

1 Do you mind if I sit here?
2 Can we have the bill, please?
3 Could you open the window, please?
4 Is it all right to turn on the radio?
5 Excuse me, can you pass me my coat, please?
6 Would you mind lending me €5 until tomorrow?

UNIT 8 RECORDING 3

1 A: I forgot to tell Jack about the meeting.
B: Shall I phone him for you?
2 A: I'm really thirsty.
B: I'll get you a drink.
3 A: Hello, IT Support? My printer isn't working.
B: OK. I'll come over and have a look.
4 A: I think I'm going to miss my train.
B: Don't worry, I'll take you to the station
5 A: This CD is great!
B: I'll lend it to you if you want.
6 A: That old lady's having trouble with her bags.
B: Shall I go over and help?
7 A: Can you give me some information about holidays in Greece?
B: Certainly. I'll get you a brochure.
8 A: Sandra loves these sandals.
B: Shall I buy her a pair for her birthday?

UNIT 8 RECORDING 4

Culture clash

In Africa, a famous food company tried to sell its baby food by advertising it with the picture of a baby on the label. They did not know that this particular country used labels only to show a picture of the food inside! When Pepsico used the slogan 'Come Alive With Pepsi' in Taiwan, they had no idea that it would be translated into Chinese as 'Pepsi brings your ancestors back from the dead.'

Misunderstandings such as these about language or about culture are sometimes comical but can also cause genuine hurt or anger. Business styles and customs vary widely in different countries and what is normal in one culture can be completely unacceptable in another. How well is your company prepared? Try this short test. Look at the following situations. What mistakes have been made?

1 You are in Paris on business. In a meeting it is very hot and you suggest to everyone that they take off their ties and roll up their sleeves.
2 A Japanese businessman asks, 'When do you want the report?' 'Yesterday!' answers the American businesswoman.
3 In an Arabic country, a group from a British company are invited to a dinner party. They all bring gifts and during the evening they continue to talk about their work.
4 A sales manager in Hong Kong is angry because his workers are always fifteen minutes late for work. He makes a new rule that they all must come on time.
5 A Spanish secretary receives an urgent request to email a report to the New York office before 2/3. She sends it on 1st March.
6 You are having a meal with Chinese colleagues in Nanjing. After the meal you use the hot towel to wipe your hands and your face.

How did you do? Did you spot the 'cultural clashes'? Well, in the first situation, French businessmen rarely take off their ties even if the weather is very hot. The idea of the American 'casual Friday' where the boss is called by his or her first name and people can wear jeans and trainers is a complete mystery to many other nationalities. In Germany, for example, colleagues call each other by their titles and surnames, (e.g. Herr, Doktor) in the workplace.

For many western countries, 'time is money' and good business equals fast business. However, in some cultures people consider that building good relationships with business partners is more important. They think in months and years and not days and hours and they find western executives impatient.

Socialising in different countries can be tricky. In Arabic countries, for example, people do not discuss business over meals. Giving gifts is another potential problem: in the UK most people take presents to a dinner party, but in many countries this is not polite because it suggests that you think the host is poor.

The Hong Kong story is true. The workers started coming on time but they also stopped exactly on time instead of working into the night as they used to do and left a great deal of work unfinished.

The Spanish secretary was a month late. She didn't realise that in America the month is written before the day, whereas in Europe the day comes first.

Finally, in the Chinese restaurant it is bad manners to wipe your face with a towel. Chinese people use it only for their hands.

So how did you do? Are you culturally aware or do you need a course in cross-cultural relationships? Whatever you do, remember that your way is not the only way and it is important to respect other people's customs.

UNIT 9 RECORDING 1

Yesterday I cleared up my house and I mean *really* cleared up my house. The room that gave the most results was my husband's 'office'. There I found: one right-footed walking boot, size 10 (he lost the other one somewhere); a garden badminton set, complete with rackets and a net (we decided to get fit last summer and played with it once); a set of *Star Wars* videos; and two small china cats someone gave me last birthday. I collected these and other 'finds', took them downstairs and logged on to www.eBay.com: the answer to all our rubbish – or 'one person's junk is another person's treasure.'

What is eBay? The simple answer is that it is the world's most popular auction house. The website says, 'eBay's mission is to provide a global trading platform where practically anyone can trade practically anything' – yes, even one right-footed boot. People can sell and buy in a range of over 300 categories, including cars and other vehicles, movies and DVDs, sporting goods, collectibles, travel, tickets, musical instruments, real estate, clothes and shoes, jewellery – the list goes on and on.

The idea came from Peter Omidyar. Born in Paris, Omidyar, moved to Washington when he was still a child. At High School he became very interested in computer programming and after graduating from Tuft University in 1988, he worked for the next few years as a computer engineer. In his free time he started eBay as a kind of hobby, originally offering the service free by word of mouth. By 1996 there was so much traffic on the site that he had to upgrade and he began charging a fee to members. Joined by a friend, Peter Skoll, and in 1988 by his dynamic CEO, Meg Whitman, he has never looked back. Even in the great dot com crashes of the late 1990s, eBay went from strength to strength. It is now one of the ten most visited online shopping sites on the internet.

If you think about it, it's a perfect internet idea. It sells connections not goods, putting buyer and seller into contact with each other. All you have to do is take an e-photo, write a description, fill out a sales form and you're in business; the world is your marketplace. Oh, and of course for each item sold, eBay gets a percentage and that is a great deal of money. Everyday there are more than 16 million items listed on eBay and 80 percent of items are sold.

Some of the more bizarre items up for offer have been a piece of French toast, partially eaten by Justin Timberlake, advertising space on a man's head, a pair of used false teeth, and 'Nothing' (the seller said he would give the profits to a local university).

One week later, I am the proud possessor of a clean and tidy home and €110 in cash. Someone even bought the boot.

UNIT 9 RECORDING 2

1 A leisure time activity is something which you enjoy doing in your free time.
2 A determined person is someone who knows what they want and works hard to get it.
3 The Jim twins were brothers whose lives were remarkably similar.
4 An archaeological site is a place where people have found important historical buildings or objects.
5 A brilliant film is one which people think is very good.
6 A confident person is someone who believes in their own ability to do something.
7 Kobe is the town in Japan where karaoke probably started.
8 A disappointing book is one which we expect to be better than it is.

UNIT 9 RECORDING 3

1 A: Good morning, Patricia speaking. How can I help?
B: Hello. I've got a problem with my tablet computer. I was working on a document this morning and it crashed three times.
A: Have you tried restarting it?
B: Yes, several times.
A: OK, well I think the best thing to do is reinstall the software. First, you need to …
2 A: Good morning, Meccaphone, George speaking.
B: Hi! I hope you can help. My touch-screen phone's gone dead.
A: How long have you had it?
B: A week.
A: You probably need to recharge the battery.
B: And another thing … I can't access the apps I've downloaded.
A: You need to access the downloads folder. Open 'settings' and scroll down the menu with your finger until you come to 'downloads'. Then touch the icon and they should be there.
B: OK, thanks!
3 A: Good morning, Print Logistics. How can I help you?
B: Morning. Our photocopier doesn't work. Every time we try to copy something, it breaks down and stops working.
A: OK, switch it off at the wall, then unplug it.
B: Hang on … oh; right, I've done that.
A: Hold down the 'print' button while you switch it back on. Can you see a menu?
B: Yes, I see it.
A: In the menu, press 'restart'. That should solve the problem.

UNIT 9 RECORDING 4

Stress on the first part	Stress on both parts
laptop	digital camera
internet addict	personal trainer
dishwasher	electric cooker
bodyguard	personal computer
recycling bin	mobile phone
energy drink	
instruction manual	
washing machine	
games console	

UNIT 9 RECORDING 5

1 A: I haven't got anything to wear.
S: But you've got some really nice clothes.
2 A: I've got no friends.
S: Come on … you've got loads of friends.
3 A: I haven't got much money.
S: You only need enough for a taxi.
4 A: There'll be too many people.
S: Oh, but only a few people are coming.
5 A: I never have anything to say.
S: Don't be silly. You've got plenty you could talk about.
6 A: I've got too much homework to do.
S: You've got a couple of hours tomorrow when you could finish it.
7 A: There isn't enough time to get ready.
S: There's lots of time – we don't need to be there until nine!

UNIT 9 RECORDING 6

1 A: Can I help at all?
B: No, thanks. I'm just looking.
2 A: How would you like to pay?
B: By credit card, please.

3 A: Can I bring it back if it isn't right?
B: Yes, that's fine. Just keep your receipt.
4 A: How did you get on with those?
B: Yes, they were OK.
5 A: Do I have to pay for delivery?
B: No, you don't. Orders over £50 are delivered free.
6 A: Have you got a product code?
B: Yes, it's XU319.
7 A: Do you have this in a size 16?
B: I'll have a look for you.
8 A: Is that including VAT?
B: No, it's not.

UNIT 10 RECORDING 1

1 sixteen percent
2 fifty thousand and twenty-five
3 one point five million
4 thirty degrees Celsius
5 one thousand four hundred and fifty square kilometres
6 a profit of twenty-one percent

UNIT 10 RECORDING 2

1 A: I've never done any salsa dancing before.
B: In that case, you may well find it best to take some lessons.
2 A: Melanie seems unhappy in her job.
B: Yes. She may well leave the company soon.
3 A: How long have Jon and Sylvie been going out with each other?
B: Almost a year now and they may well get married next year.
4 A: I am phoning to check my flight. It's BA 2517.
B: Conditions are very poor at the moment and they may well cancel the flight.
5 A: When is your driving test?
B: In two days' time. I feel OK about the practical but I may well fail the written exam.
6 A: It's very cold, isn't it? Have you seen the weather forecast today?
B: Yes. It may well snow later.

UNIT 10 RECORDING 3

1 A: Brazil are likely to win the World Cup. (may well)
B: Brazil may well win the World Cup.
2 A: I'm sure we won't have time to do any sightseeing. (definitely)
B: We definitely won't have time to do any sightseeing.
3 A: It'll probably rain before the end of the day. (likely)
B: It's likely to rain before the end of the day.
4 A: Perhaps my friend Mari will be a famous actress one day. (could)
B: My friend Mari could be a famous actress one day.
5 A: My boss is very unlikely to agree to the pay rise. (almost certainly)
B: My boss almost certainly won't agree to the pay rise.
6 A: I think you'll recognise my sister when you see her. (probably)
B: You'll probably recognise my sister when you see her.
7 A: We probably won't get back from the theatre before midnight. (likely)
B: We aren't likely to get back from the theatre before midnight.
8 A: I'm sure that our teacher will give us a lot of homework for the weekend. (almost certainly)
B: Our teacher will almost certainly give us a lot of homework for the weekend.

UNIT 10 RECORDING 4

A A: I can't decide whether to have the baby in hospital or not.
B: Well, I 'd go into hospital, especially as it's your first baby.
A: Yes, you're probably right.
B: Have you decided on a name yet?
A: Yes – if it's a boy, we'll call him Tom, and if it's a girl, Sara.
B A: Why aren't you going to your classes?
B: Because they're so boring: I'd go if they were more interesting. And I always get bad marks.
A: Well, that's not surprising: if you spent less time playing computer games and worked harder, you wouldn't have so many problems.

UNIT 10 RECORDING 5

1 I'd move to Antarctica if ...
2 I'll go on holiday next summer if ...
3 I'll speak to my mother next week if ...
4 If I won the lottery, I'd ...
5 I'll go to bed early tonight if ...
6 I'd stop studying English if ...

UNIT 10 RECORDING 6

Stuck on a desert island?

Post 1 Steve, USA

Hi everyone,

What would you miss most and least if you were stuck on a desert island? For me it would be the changing seasons, especially the fall in New England. Sure, it would be fantastic to have non-stop sun, but I'd miss the colours of the seasons. I guess this will sound stupid but I'd probably miss the rain too! I wouldn't miss getting up at six every day to go to work, though!

What about you?

Post 2 Tomas, Germany

Good question, Steve. I think I'd miss the pastries and different types of bread, and shopping at the local markets, and sausages, although I suppose I could try and make my own. So, yeah, the food. I'd miss the food most. What would I miss least? My mobile – I'd like to be completely uncontactable – at least for a little while.

Post 3 Paola, Italy

I would miss the company of people because I know I'd like to have someone to share experiences with. For instance, if there was a fantastic sunrise, I'd want someone to be there to enjoy it with me. I'm a sociable sort of person and I'd go mad on my own. And I definitely wouldn't miss junk mail – I hate coming home every evening and finding a pile of junk mail in my post box.

Post 4 Miko, Japan

Hi,

I would miss Manga cartoons, the internet and Japanese food, like nori, sushi and Japanese beef. I'd also miss TV shows and shopping for clothes ... and my two dogs. In fact, I'd miss everything.

Post 5 Roger, UK

I would miss my daily newspaper and listening to the news on the TV and radio. I'd feel very cut off if I didn't know what was happening in the world. If you gave me a radio, then I'd be perfectly happy to live on a desert island for the rest of my life. What I'd miss least would be traffic jams in the city, particularly my journey to work.

Post 6 Jayne, Canada

Why hasn't anyone mentioned their family? I'd be lost without my husband and two kids. They're the most important things for me. Maybe coffee, too. I can't get started in the morning without a cup of black coffee. I wouldn't miss doing the housework. Just think, no more cleaning or washing-up! And it'd be good to be able to relax as much as I wanted.

Post 7 Jaime, Mexico

It would have to be music. I couldn't live without my music! I wouldn't miss going to school at all or doing homework!

UNIT 11 RECORDING 1

1 You have to leave your keys at reception when you go out of the hotel.
2 I think people should spend more time with their families and less time at work.
3 Passengers aren't allowed to walk around the plane when it is taking off.
4 Candidates are allowed to take a dictionary into the exam, but they can't take in a grammar book.
5 You can't drive a car unless you're over 17.
6 You look really tired. I think you ought to take a day off.
7 Monday's a holiday so we don't have to go to school until Tuesday.
8 You mustn't ride a bicycle on the motorway – it's very dangerous.
9 Guests can have breakfast any time between 7:00 and 9:00 a.m.
10 You must sign your name in this book when you enter or leave the building.

UNIT 11 RECORDING 2

1 You can't park there.
2 Students mustn't arrive late.
3 You ought to talk to her about it.
4 We have to be there 30 minutes before it starts.
5 I'm not allowed to copy this text.
6 You shouldn't say things like that.
7 You don't have to wear jeans, but you can if you want to.
8 You can't use your phone in here.

UNIT 11 RECORDING 3

1 When 15-year-old Mario Silva refused to cut his hair because he wanted to look like his favourite film star, his father pulled out a gun and threatened to shoot him. 'My husband had been telling Mario to get his hair cut for the last two years and they had an argument,' said his wife.

Fernando Silva was arrested and will appear in court next week. Meanwhile, Mario has decided to sue him and to ask to be formally separated from his parents. 'I don't feel safe in the house anymore,' he told our reporter.

2 A Jamaican woman sued her parents after falling down the stairs of their home during a visit. Beatrice, who was in her early 20s, said that her parents had been negligent because they 'failed to look after the carpet on the stairs.' As a result of the fall, she suffered serious and permanent injuries when she tripped over the carpet in August 2002. She was awarded $1,000 in damages at a court in Kingston.

3 In 1996, 17-year-old Olympic gold medallist Dominique Moceneau left home and asked to become a legal adult and to be in control of her own money. She said that her father, Dumitru Moceneau, had taken all her winnings and left her with no money and that her parents had robbed her of her childhood by pushing her so hard to become a gymnast. After hearing her complaints, a Texan court granted her independence from her parents.

4 A Canadian actress is suing her parents for making her fat. Tina Stowe, a well-known TV star in Canada, says that her mother, Lisa, kept five jars of cookies in the house in places where a child could easily find them and used to make the situation worse by telling her she was prettier than the other girls in her school. Stowe has said that her mother should have married a more suitable partner, preferably someone of a slimmer build. Stowe will appear in court next month.

UNIT 11 RECORDING 4

1 **A:** Children have an easy life these days.
B: Why do you say that?

2 **A:** People who get caught shoplifting should be sent to prison.
B: I don't know about that. In my opinion it depends on what they steal.

3 **A:** It seems to me that people who come from broken families usually become criminals.
B: Well, I take your point. It's sometimes true, but to be honest I don't really agree.
There are lots of examples where the opposite is true.

4 **A:** I think he's innocent.
B: What do you mean? They caught him on camera!

5 **A:** In my opinion, prison never works as a punishment.
B: It *never* works? You have to remember that in some cases it's the only option to protect the public.

6 **A:** What do you think about this new law on immigration?
B: I don't know about you, but I think it's a bit harsh.

UNIT 12 RECORDING 1

1 You should have read the instructions first.
2 We could walk to the party.
3 The hotel doesn't look very nice in the photos. I wouldn't have stayed there.
4 You could have invited Sarah to your party.
5 I think we're lost. We shouldn't have turned left at the traffic lights.
6 That computer was so cheap. Why didn't you buy it? I would have

Answer key

UNIT 1

1
2 How is your job going?
3 When did you get here?
4 How is all your family?
5 How do you do?
6 Did you have a good journey here?
7 How are things with you?
8 Where are you staying while you are here?

2
2 Is
3 does
4 do
5 Was
6 did
7 Has
8 Are

3
a
2 j
3 f
4 c
5 i
6 a
7 d
8 b
9 h
10 e

4
2 Do you live with your family?
3 What page are they looking at?
4 Where exactly does he live?
5 How was your holiday?
6 What time do you usually get up?
7 Does your English teacher speak your language?
8 Where did you go to university?

5
2 Can you **write** 'customer' on the board, please?
3 What's **the** English word for this?
4 Which page **are we** on?
5 **Has** anybody got a spare pen?
6 Can you say **that again**, please?
7 What **is** tonight's homework?
8 How **do** you spell 'journey'?
9 What **does** 'colleague' **mean**?

6
a
2 How do you spell your name?
3 Have you got any brothers and sisters?
4 No, I haven't.
5 Which one would you like?
6 Does your mother speak English?
7 Yes, actually she does.
8 How was your weekend?
9 What's your date of birth?
10 What time do you usually get up in the morning?

7
2 parent
3 relative
4 stranger
5 cousin
6 acquaintance
7 classmate
8 colleague
9 stepmother
10 neighbour

8
a
1 B
2 C
3 A
b
A
2 own
3 help
4 do, look
5 do, do
6 Does, rain
7 does, belong
8 know
9 own
10 don't know
11 want
12 Do, believe
13 has
14 doesn't have
15 spend
16 don't drink
17 get
18 comes

9
2 are staying
3 is having
4 are getting
5 are eating
6 aren't getting
7 aren't setting
8 're spending
9 is, suffering
10 are, breathing
11 are dying
12 are, watching
13 'm cleaning
14 'm getting
15 are, using
16 are, talking

10
2 is going
3 Do you smoke
4 do you work
5 do
6 'm working
7 do you relax
8 sit
9 Are you doing
10 don't know
11 're suffering
12 want

11
a
1 Annette's
2 Dan's
3 Charlotte's
b
1 Mary
2 Charlotte
3 Annette
4 Kimberley
5 Mary
6 Ricky
7 Mary
8 Annette

12
2 i, doing paperwork
3 f, going on social networking sites
4 a, tidying up
5 j, looking after children
6 d, going shopping
7 h, playing video games
8 b, commuting
9 g, texting
10 e, doing nothing

13
a
b 1
c 3
b
2 Of course I remember you – how could I forget?
3 It was great to hear all your news
4 You look great in your photos, you haven't changed a bit.
5 You must tell me all about him!
6 As for my news, well, I'm also very busy these days.
7 It's funny that you asked about Tom.
8 As for my parents, ...
9 It would be fantastic to see you again, and I can't wait to meet Hendrik!
10 Great to hear from you.

14
a
2 Don't you?
3 Haven't you?
4 Did you?
5 Are you?
6 Was it?
7 Did she?
8 Do you?
b
2 a
3 f
4 d
5 h
6 g
7 e
8 c

UNIT 2

1
2 Did, ring
3 didn't want
4 Did, go
5 stayed
6 cooked
7 Did, hear
8 happened
9 rained
10 got
11 didn't, tell
12 got
13 introduced
14 forgot

2
2 were you talking
3 wasn't concentrating
4 was he doing, was buying
5 wasn't listening
6 was moving
7 were having
8 were we making, were putting

3
2 He was playing football and he fell over.
3 We were sunbathing at the weekend and we stayed out too long.
4 He was walking in the rain and he got very wet.
5 They were staying in Florida when there was a terrible storm.
6 She was travelling home from work and she left it on the bus.

4
2 was working
3 didn't hear
4 was talking
5 went
6 was
7 was training
8 broke
9 spent

5
2 We were driving home and another car stopped suddenly and we crashed into the back of it.
3 Was the other car all right?
4 Yes, luckily we weren't going very fast.
5 What did you do to your hand?
6 I burnt it.
7 I was ironing a shirt, and the phone rang, and I put the iron down on my hand by mistake!

6 a
3 travelled, 2
4 looked, 1
5 reminded, 3
6 visited, 3
7 phoned, 1
8 changed, 1
9 practised, 2
10 opened, 2
11 improved, 2
12 received, 2
13 repeated, 3
14 answered, 2

7
2 respect
3 encouraged
4 pocket money
5 got into trouble, punished
6 praised, gave confidence
7 argued, tell off
8 strict

8
2 My friends and I didn't use to go to the gym every week, but now we ~~go to the gym every week~~. do
3 My boyfriend used to be a terrible cook, but he isn't a ~~terrible cook~~ anymore.
4 There used to be a lot of traffic in my city, and there still is ~~a lot of traffic~~.
5 I didn't use to know how to send text messages, but now I ~~know how to send text messages~~. do
6 When I was younger, I would spend a lot of time reading, but now I don't ~~spend a lot of time reading~~.
7 I didn't use to like spiders and I still don't ~~like spiders~~!
8 My family didn't use to go overseas for our holidays, but now we ~~go overseas for our holidays~~. do
9 I used to be very shy but I'm not ~~shy~~ any longer.
10 In my old job, I would often stay in the office late, but now I don't ~~stay in the office late~~.

9 a
She used to sing in a band.
She used to ride a motorbike.
She used to travel all over the world.
She didn't use to design sports clothes.
She didn't use to be married to a famous footballer.
She didn't use to have two children.
She didn't use to live in Italy.
b
She still has long hair.
She doesn't sing in a band anymore / any longer.
She still keeps fit.
She doesn't ride a motorbike anymore / any longer.
She still earns a lot of money.
She doesn't travel all over the world anymore.

10 a
A2, B6, C9, D5
b
language 8
animals 10
transport 2
countries 1
politics 6
drink 7
food 4
teachers 9
kitchen appliances 5

11
2 of
3 him
4 about
5 to phone
6 it
7 meeting
8 to give
9 when we got
10 about

12 a
2 remember
3 forget
4 recognise
5 remind
6 forget
7 remember
8 recognise
9 remember
10 remind

13 a
2 while/when
3 when
4 while/when
5 while/when
6 when
7 when
8 while/when
b
2 Unfortunately, while/when I was talking to Guy on the phone, the cat walked over my shirt, so I had to iron another one.
3 While/When I was walking to the station it started snowing and I got cold.
4 The train was delayed because it started snowing and when it finally arrived I was frozen!
5 I fell asleep while/when I was sitting on the train and missed the station.
6 I got off at the next station and decided to walk to Kyra's house. When I reached the end of the road I realised I was lost.
7 I didn't have my mobile so I looked for a phone box to call a taxi.
8 When I arrived at Kyra's house it was nearly midnight and people were going home!

Answer key

UNIT 3

1
2 The **easiest** way
3 more expensive **than** the train
4 worst
5 **most** popular
6 hotter
7 **in** the world
8 busier
9 further
10 **the** best deals

2
2 the biggest
3 the most central
4 better
5 further
6 friendlier
7 quieter
8 the most expensive
9 more crowded
10 the most successful

3
2 the second most popular
3 far better looking
4 the least reliable
5 one of the easiest
6 a little bit lighter
7 a lot bigger
8 much better
9 a little more reliable
10 by far the best

4
2 a mosque
3 a monument
4 a skyscraper
5 a bay
6 a harbour
7 a canal
8 farmland
9 a hill
10 a factory
11 ancient ruins
12 a bridge
13 a festival
14 a palace
15 a waterfall

5 **a**
1 b Luxury Under Water
c White Shark Heaven, Mexico
d Wilderness Husky Adventure
2 Luxury Under Water, White Shark Heaven, Mexico
3 Storm Chasing, The Final Frontier: 3,400 kph

b
1 six (train, plane, van, sledge, snowmobile, boat)
2 four (The Final Frontier, Wilderness Husky Adventure, Storm Chasing, White Shark Heaven)
3 Because the temperatures are so extreme – very hot or very cold.
4 The curvature of the earth.
5 no ('the chase could take you anywhere ...')
6 Have a traditional sauna.
7 Luxury Under Water.
8 no ('for divers, non-divers and tuna fishermen')

6
2 to
3 completely
4 as
5 similar
6 different
7 more, less
8 slightly
9 the, as

7
2 The Manor Hotel isn't as expensive as the Park Hotel.
3 Savewell supermarket has more customers a day than Pricerite supermarket.
4 There are fewer trains in the afternoon than in the morning.
5 The furniture in my sister's flat is similar to Tim's.
6 The Guggenheim Museum in New York is different from the Guggenheim Museum in Bilbao.
7 My flat's (exactly) the same as Phil's (flat).

8 **a and b**
2 the (/ə/) third largest
3 similar to (/ə/)
4 not as (/ə/) good as (/ə/)
5 fewer (/ə/)
6 different (/ə/) from (/ə/)

9
2 historic
3 touristy
4 romantic
5 crowded
6 poor
7 colourful
8 polluted
9 expensive
10 dirty
11 arty
12 dangerous

10 Positive: friendly, cosmopolitan, modern, colourful, spectacular, peaceful, smart, romantic, lively
Negative: dangerous, crowded, poor, touristy, polluted, expensive, dirty

11 **a**
2 Could you tell me what time the train arrives?
3 Do you know how much it will cost?
4 Do you know where I have to change?
5 Could you tell me which platform the train to Paris goes from?
6 Do you know which bus this is?
7 Do you know when the next one is?
8 Could you tell me how I get to the airport?

12 **a**

Dear Pete and Sarah,

We're having a great time here in the Big Apple.

The weather **is** brilliant – hot and sunny. **We** spent most of today shopping – **there are** fantastic department stores here: **my** credit card's not looking too healthy! **We're** hoping to do some sightseeing tomorrow – Fifth Avenue, Times Square, etc. **The** nightlife **is** also incredible ... nobody seems to go to bed!

We'll be back in a couple of weeks,

love Sue and Joe

x x x x

We usually leave out: pronouns (*we*, *you*, etc.), definite articles (*the*), the verb *to be*. We sometimes leave out possessive adjectives (*my*, *your*, etc.).

b

Dear Sam and Julie,

We arrived here a couple of days ago – the hotel is small but comfortable, but the food is not great. We're going on a tour of the whole city tomorrow, then we're planning to try some typical pasta dishes for dinner. We hope your family are all well, we'll see you in September.

Love Mark and Tim

UNIT 4

1 a
3 worn
4 read
5 drunk
6 kept
7 put
8 torn
9 rung
10 got
11 told
12 lent
13 driven
14 eaten
15 taught
16 hit
17 thrown
18 won

b
2 've kept
3 've thrown
4 've worn
5 've torn
6 's hit
7 have, told
8 hasn't broken
9 've lent
10 has, driven
11 've put
12 have, known
13 's eaten
14 's drunk

2
2 it's been
3 've already had
4 've done
5 started
6 formed
7 've spent
8 played
9 didn't start
10 found
11 was
12 got
13 went
14 've just agreed

3
2 Carrie's a really close friend – we**'ve known** each other for ages.
3 Hello, er ... sorry, **I've forgotten** your name.
5 Oh, that's a nice watch. How long **have** you **had** it?
8 I see your team's in the final. **Have** they ever **won** the cup?
9 We **haven't played** tennis together since the summer.

4 a
2 have been
3 've never stayed
4 've lived
5 moved
6 've met
7 've had
8 've been
9 was
10 had
11 took
12 's gone

5 a
2 Did Stefano come to class yesterday?
3 I've done all the exercises in this unit so far.
4 She's only seen her brother twice in the last ten years.
5 I started learning English in 2010.
6 He's lived here since 2005.
7 What was your favourite game when you were young?

6 a
2 b
3 b
4 a
5 b
6 a

7 a
a 5
b 6
c 8
d 2
e 3
f 4
g 1
h 7

b
1 Because he can act in mainstream Hollywood and 'out of the ordinary' projects.
2 Acting a role which doesn't have any part of yourself in it.
3 Because his musical career wasn't successful and he needed money.
4 Because he persuaded him to try acting.
5 His character was eaten by his bed.
6 He was popular with teenagers. (he was a 'teen' idol)
7 He directed, co-wrote and starred in it.
8 Tim Burton.
9 He has still got the tattoo, but it doesn't say 'Winona'.
10 Geoffrey Rush.

8
2 left
3 got
4 lost
5 fell
6 got
7 bringing
8 changed
9 moved
10 got
11 leave
12 go
13 passed
14 graduated
15 got
16 bought
17 retire

9
2 's been talking
3 've been using
4 's been going
5 Has, been crying
6 haven't been working
7 's been phoning
8 has, been raining
9 've been looking
10 's been studying

10
2 for six months
3 for a year
4 since last night
5 for two weeks
6 for months
7 since this time last year
8 since her operation
9 for ages
10 since 1997

11
2 's broken
3 's had
4 's been waiting
5 've been going
6 's been practising
7 been dieting
8 has decided
9 've really enjoyed

12
2 Katalin has been writing novels since she retired.
3 Sue and Jenny have known each other for years.
4 Finally! We've been waiting for you for two hours!
5 The band has played over 100 gigs since they formed.
6 Wolf has been working really hard since he got promoted.
7 I've been a member of the party for 20 years.
8 Gina has been living with her parents for a while to save money.
9 She's been training for the marathon since July.
10 I've been skiing since I was a child.

13
2 courageous
3 obsessive
4 charming
5 determined
6 talented
7 self-confident
8 egotistical
9 dedicated
10 original
11 ruthless
12 inspiring

14
2 courageous
3 obsessive
4 charming
5 dedicated
6 talented
7 self-confident
8 egotistical
9 determined
10 original
11 ruthless
12 inspiring

Answer key

UNIT 5

1
2 profit
3 distractions
4 improvement
5 imaginative
6 knowledgeable
7 failure
8 produce

2 **a** and **b**
2 4, experience
3 3, productive
4 4, profitable
5 3, distraction
6 5, imagination
7 2, failure
8 3, imagine
9 4, experienced
10 3, improvement
11 4, knowledgeable
12 1, know

3
2 's he going to do?
3 I am
4 are going to see
5 'm not going to think
6 Is she going to marry
7 are they going to build
8 we aren't

4
2 What are you doing in the afternoon?
3 Well, I'm playing squash until three o'clock, then I've got a tutorial.
4 Are you doing anything in the evening?
5 Well, he's seeing patients all morning.
6 No, I'm afraid he's having the afternoon off.
7 Ah, Celia, what time am I having lunch with Gary Parsons?
8 You're leaving at two to visit the factory in Stanmore.

5
2 'll need
3 Will you be
4 won't like
5 will they send
6 'll get
7 'll pass
8 won't take

6
2 They're due to arrive at about six.
3 Yes, we're hoping to move next month.
4 I know, she's about to take her driving test.
5 Well, I'm thinking of buying a new car.
6 I'm intending to spend the night there.

7
2 a
3 c
4 a
5 c
6 b
7 b
8 c
9 a
10 a

8
2 good with numbers
3 competitive
4 well-organised
5 special training
6 well-paid
7 long hours
8 qualifications

9
b 3 get
c 6 receive
d 2 sends
e 1 is/'s
f 5 start

10
2 Let's stop (now) before it gets dark .
3 You won't get the job unless you can offer something extra.
4 I'd like to see that film as soon as it comes out.
5 I'll wait with you until the taxi comes.
6 You'll be here by lunchtime if you take the 9 a.m. flight.
7 You'll see the bus stop on your right when you come out of the station.
8 I want to go to bed as soon as I get home.
9 I'll book a table at the Wharf Bistro unless you want to go somewhere else.

11 **a**
1 singer
2 chef
3 crossword puzzle writer
4 flight attendant

b
2 T
3 F
4 F
5 T
6 T
1 T
8 T
9 F
10 F
11 F
12 T

12 **a**
1 letter A
2 letter B

b

A
2 paid
3 responsibilities
4 skills
5 asset
6 achieved

B
1 confirm
2 since
3 As
4 numerous
5 further
6 hesitate

13 **a**
2 speaking
3 could I speak to
4 available
5 calling
6 to call me back
7 take your number
8 Thank you. Goodbye

UNIT 6

1
2 had forgotten
3 had made
4 had, sold
5 hadn't had
6 had left
7 had met
8 hadn't travelled
9 hadn't done
10 hadn't won

2
2 a
3 a
4 b
5 a
6 b
7 b
8 a

3
2 was; had left
3 felt had; 'd had
4 had stopped, got
5 had known, asked
6 married, didn't realise, 'd been married
7 hadn't seen, felt
8 sang, 'd never heard
9 'd written, posted
10 was; had eaten

4
a
2 A
3 B
4 B
5 A
6 B
7 A
8 B

5
a
2 was
3 lived
4 was
5 wasn't seeing
6 had never been
7 had been
8 would be

6
2 it would rain overnight
3 he's doing / he was doing very well at maths
4 I could be anything I wanted to be
5 fifty-six people have / had been killed in a train crash
6 the world was flat
7 people in Brazil use / used the internet more than anyone
8 he'd just got married
9 he practised / he'd practised eight hours a day
10 she was working with some great people

7
a
2 She wanted to know what my job was.
3 She asked me when I had arrived in London.
4 She wanted to know if I lived in Rome.
5 She asked me where I was living in London.
6 She asked me how long I'd been learning English.
7 She wanted to know if I liked England.
8 She asked me if I'd been to London before.
b
2 What is your job? / What do you do?
3 When did you arrive in London?
4 Do you live in Rome?
5 Where are you living in London?
6 How long have you been learning English?
7 Do you like England?
8 Have you been to London before?

8
a
2 He asked me if I was here on holiday.
3 He asked me if I was travelling alone.
4 He asked me if I had packed my suitcases myself.
5 He asked me if I had been to the USA before.
6 He asked me how long I would be in the country.
7 He asked me if I knew anyone in San Francisco.
8 He asked me where I was going to stay.
9 He asked me how much money I had with me.

9
a
4 Pat's father told her / said she should be more polite.
5 Danny told me / said he was going to the USA.
6 Tell your brother that you're sorry.
8 Could you tell me / say your name again, please?
b
2 told, off
3 tell, the truth
4 saying, goodbye
5 said, sorry
6 say, thank you
7 tell, about
8 said, no
9 tell, difference
10 told, what

10
1 D
2 A
3 E
4 B
5 C

11
2 fortunately
3 gradually
4 Surprisingly
5 suddenly
6 Unfortunately
7 obviously
8 eventually

12
2 found
3 Then
4 fell
5 new wife
6 enough
7 told
8 for
9 beautiful
10 a lot of gold
11 more fabric
12 thinner
13 could
14 more
15 did not
16 the hunter
17 surprise
18 her arms
19 cannot stay
20 flew

Answer key

UNIT 7

1
2 weather forecast
3 murder mystery
4 documentary
5 travel news
6 game show
7 talent show
8 phone-in
9 reality show
10 sitcom
11 soap opera
12 cookery programme

2 a
2 shocking
3 disappointed
4 confused
5 shocked
6 annoyed
7 pleased
8 inspiring
9 disappointing

3
2 embarrassing
3 annoyed
4 inspired
5 irritating
6 confusing
7 shocked
8 frustrating

4
2 have
3 be
4 has
5 were
6 was
7 are
8 is
9 had
10 are

5
2 When was the car stolen?
3 Where are tickets for the concert sold?
4 Where will the new hospital be built?
5 Who was the article written by?
6 Why has the open air concert been cancelled?
7 Where is Portuguese spoken?
8 What was Napoleon known as?
9 Who was the film directed by?
10 How many people have been injured?

6
2 was found
3 have been stolen
4 are, being held / will, be held
5 are not to be sold
6 Was, built
7 is not included
8 Are, frozen

7
2 are made
3 export
4 are worn
5 was
6 were written
7 was
8 will be givens
9 has been redesigned
10 open
11 comes
12 are checked

8 a
2 freezing
3 terrified
4 ridiculous
5 hilarious
6 tragic
7 astonished
8 boiling

9 a
2 D
3 D
4 S
5 D
6 S
7 S
8 S

10 a
2 a comedy show
3 a classical concert
4 an opera
5 a play
6 a TV drama
7 a pop video
8 a TV drama
9 a comedy show
10 a musical
11 a ballet
12 a play
13 a rock concert

b
2 lyrics
3 plot
4 cast
5 set
6 special effects
7 scenery
8 orchestra

11 a
1 B
2 C
3 A

b
2 F
3 F
4 T
5 T
6 F
7 T
8 F
9 T
10 F

12 a
2 Would you like to come?, I'm sorry
3 when you get there
4 I'd love to!
5 What about meeting, I'll see you there
6 Are you free, I'm having

13 a
1 C, E
2 F, B
3 A, D

b

Inviting:
I was wondering if you'd like to come ...
Let me know as soon as you can.
Could you possibly come to ...
I do hope you can come.

Accepting an invitation:
I'd love to come.
Yes, I think I can make it.

Refusing an invitation:
I'm afraid ...
I won't be able to come.
What a shame – some other time perhaps?

UNIT 8

1
2 Yes
3 Yes
4 Yes
5 Yes
6 No
7 Yes

2
2 Do you mind if I sit here?
3 Could you speak more slowly, please?
4 Would you mind looking after my bag for a minute?
5 Could I possibly borrow $20?
6 Would you mind turning down your music?

3 a
2 Would you **mind** helping me with my suitcase?
3 Could **you** pass the salt, please?
4 Would you **bring** us the bill, please?
5 Do you mind **if I go now**?
6 **Would** you mind getting me some milk?
7 Could I **possibly** have a look at your newspaper?
8 Would you mind **answering** my phone while I'm out?

4
2 Do you think I could borrow your camera?
3 Could you say that again?
4 Would you mind checking this letter?
5 Would you turn the radio down?
6 Do you think you could lend me ten euros?
7 Do you mind if I give you my essay a day late?
8 Could I possibly use your computer?
9 Is it OK if I tell you tomorrow?

5 a
2 B
3 B
4 A
5 B
6 A

6 a
2 Shall I get you a drink?
3 OK, I'll come over and have a look.
4 Don't worry, I'll take you to the station.
5 I'll lend it to you if you want.
6 Shall I go over and help her?
7 Certainly. I'll get you a brochure.
8 Shall I buy her a pair for her birthday?

7
1 B: Yes very – I'll take them.
2 A: I've got a problem with my shower. It isn't working.
B: I'll send someone up straightaway. Which room is it?
3 A: There's a problem with the time of my flight, I'm afraid.
B: OK, shall I see if I can change it for you?
4 A: Hi! Nice to see you. Come in and have a coffee.
B: OK, but I've got a meeting later so I'll need to leave by 11.
5 A: Are you ready to order?
B: Yes, I'll have the fish.
6 A: Has Mrs Williams in the Accounts Department returned from lunch yet?
B: Yes, she has. Shall I put you through?
7 A: Is there anything good on TV tonight?
B: I don't know – shall I have a look in the newspaper?

8
2 'll walk
3 are going to spend
4 'll go
5 'm going to visit
6 'll see
7 'll buy
8 'm going to do
9 'll throw
10 'll give

9
2 pick, up
3 refused, pay
4 went out, date
5 hugged, each other
6 took, home
9 insisted, driving
7 invited, to her party
8 shake, hands
9 insisted, driving
10 share, bill

10
2 The company representative **insisted** on paying for lunch.
3 No, we're just friends, we didn't go out **on** a date or anything like that.
4 You live near me so I'll **pick** you up on the way, if you want.
5 I'm afraid I'll have to **refuse** your kind invitation. I'll be holiday.
6 Little Johnny! Come and **kiss** grandma on both cheeks!
7 It's not safe for you to walk round here at night. Don't worry, I'll **take** you home.
8 Ronnie's so mean. He never even offers to **pay** when we go out.
9 Did you hear about that footballer who refused to shake **hands** before the game?
10 You don't have to pay just because you're a man. Let's **share** the bill.

11 a
a 3
b 8
c 2
d 5
e 1
f 4
g 6
h 7

b
2 T
3 T
4 F
5 T
6 F
7 F
8 T
9 T
10 F

12
2 In China it's considered rude to use a hot towel to wipe your face.
3 Germans don't tend to call colleagues by their first names.
4 In Japan it's good manners to build relationships slowly when doing business.
5 In many Arabic countries it's unacceptable to talk about business during meals.
6 In the UK it's important to take a gift to a dinner party.
7 In Spain it isn't usual to write 2nd July as 7/2.
8 In the USA it's perfectly normal for people to wear casual clothes on Fridays.

13 a
2 It's **considered** rude to show the bottom of your feet.
3 It's **unacceptable** to touch someone's head.
4 It's **perfectly** normal to wear jeans in an office.
5 It's good **manners** to hold the door open for someone.
6 It's important **to say** sorry if you are in someone's way.
7 On the **whole**, it's OK to blow your nose in public.
8 On the whole, it's acceptable **for** men and women to share the bill when they go out.
9 **It** is bad manners to laugh without covering your mouth.
10 It's **usual** to take a present when you go to someone's house for dinner.

Answer key

UNIT 9

1 a

1 b　　3 a
2 c　　4 c

b

1 (After paying a fee to become a member,) You have to take an e-photo, write a description and fill out a sales form.
2 a sporting goods
  b cars and other vehicles
  c real estate
  d collectibles
3 By word of mouth (people told each other about it)
4 In the late 1990s
5 No
6 Meg Whitman
7 They get a 'cut' (a percentage) of each sale.
8 Yes

2 a

2 e who　　6 b who
3 g whose　　7 d where
4 a where　　8 f which
5 h which

3 someone (who) I work with
the thing (that) I liked most

4 a and b

2 a This is the balcony where we had breakfast every morning ...
  b ... and this is the sea which/that was right in front of our apartment.
3 a This is a beach café which/that stayed open till three in the morning ...
  b ... and this is the man who/that owned it.
4 a This is a fish restaurant where we had excellent meals ...
  b ... and this is a local woman whose name I can't remember.
5 a This is one day (when) we went on a boat trip ...
  b ... and these are the men whose boat we borrowed.
6 a This is a market which/that was open every Wednesday ...
  b ... and this is me wearing a hat (which/that) I bought there.

5 a

2 restarting　　8 breaks down
3 reinstall, software　　9 switch it off
4 recharge　　10 unplug
5 scroll down　　11 Hold down
6 touch the icon　　12 press
7 doesn't work

6 a

stress on the first part	**stress on both parts**
laptop	digital camera
internet addict	personal trainer
dishwasher	electric cooker
bodyguard	personal computer
recycling bin	mobile phone
energy drink	
instruction manual	
washing machine	
games console	

7 a

countable singular: banana, chair, person, price, ring, storm, vegetable
countable plural: children, people, potatoes
uncountable: fruit, information, jewellery, milk, money, news, petrol, pollution, rice, sugar, traffic, weather

b

2 isn't　　7 Is
3 was　　8 was
4 are　　9 is
5 is　　10 was
6 is

8 a

2 d A: I've got no friends.
  S: Come on ... you've got loads of friends.
3 f A: I haven't got much money.
  S: You only need enough for a taxi.
4 g A: There'll be too many people.
  S: Oh, but only a few people are coming.
5 c A: I never have anything to say.
  S: Don't be silly. You've got plenty you could talk about.
6 a A: I've got too much homework to do.
  S: You've got a couple of hours tomorrow when you could finish it.
7 b A: There isn't enough time to get ready.
  S: There's lots of time – we don't need to be there until nine!

9

2 a **little** salt　　8 plenty **of** things
3 too **much** noise　　9 **a** lot of / lots
4 **enough** food　　10 **any**
5 not **much** parking space　　11 loads **of**
6 **not** many　　12 **no** money
7 lot **of** support

10

2 They're both made of glass.
3 They're both made of metal.
4 They're both rectangular.
5 They're both used for sticking.
6 They've both got batteries.
7 They're both round.
8 They're both made of wool.

11 a

2 How would you like to pay?
3 Can I bring it back if it isn't right?
4 How did you get on with those?
5 Do I have to pay for delivery?
6 Have you got a product code?
7 Do you have this in a size 16?
8 Is that including VAT?

b

b 4　　f 7
c 1　　g 2
d 3　　h 6
e 8

12 a

2 I don't suppose you've found it
3 could you post it
4 let me know how much the postage is
5 I am writing to enquire whether
6 I do hope it has been found
7 I would be grateful if you could send it
8 I will of course pay for postage

UNIT 10

1 a
2 50,025
3 1.5 million
4 30°C
5 1,450 km²
6 a profit of 21%
b
2 twelve thousand, two hundred and sixty-five dollars
3 fifteen square metres
4 three hundred and five thousand euros
5 thirty degrees Celsius
6 seventy kilometres an hour
7 ten million
8 four point three

2 2 She'll love it
3 I won't win
4 It won't take long
5 There will be
6 you'll arrive
7 The coach won't go
8 Will you be there?
9 It'll definitely rain
10 You'll probably

3 2 aren't likely to eat
3 isn't likely to play
4 is likely to be
5 aren't likely to improve
6 aren't likely to sleep
7 are likely to experience
8 aren't likely to arrive
9 is likely to have
10 is likely to get

4 a
2 may well leave
3 may well get married
4 may well cancel
5 may well fail
6 may well snow

5 2 Carlos probably won't pass his exam.
3 Teresa may well decide to stay in New York.
4 Sandy isn't likely to get the job.
5 I'll almost certainly do a computing course next year.
6 We could be late so don't wait for us.
7 We probably won't go away this weekend.
8 There are likely to be loads of people on the beach.
9 Jamie almost certainly won't pass his test.
10 Robots are unlikely to become more intelligent than humans.

6 a
2 We definitely won't have time to do any sightseeing.
3 It's likely to rain before the end of the day.
4 My friend Mari could be a famous actress one day.
5 My boss almost certainly won't agree to the pay rise.
6 You'll probably recognise my sister when you see her.
7 We aren't likely to get back from the theatre before midnight.
8 Our teacher will almost certainly give us a lot of homework for the weekend.

7 a
2 decrease ↓
3 go up ↑
4 get better ↑
5 fall ↓
6 become less (+ adjective) ↓
7 increase ↑
8 deteriorate ↓
9 get worse ↓
10 go down ↑
11 improve ↓
12 rise ↑
b
2 decreased / fallen / gone down
3 risen / increased / gone up
4 gone up / increased / risen
5 improved / got much better
6 become more difficult / deteriorated / got worse
7 become
8 decreases / falls / goes down
9 goes up / gets better / increases

8 a
2 would, do, tried
3 broke down, would, get out
4 Would, know, cut
5 knew, would, tell
6 Would, feel
7 Would, move, had
8 Would, eat
9 would, do, found
10 offered, would, do

b

a 8	d 3	g 5
b 4	e 7	h 2
c 7	f 9	i 6

9 a
2 's
3 'll call
4 's
5 'd / would go
6 were
7 spent
8 worked
9 wouldn't have

10 2 he'd start a business
3 if he was taller
4 if she trusted you more
5 would you take revenge
6 I would take the day off work
7 if it was on fire
8 would you live
9 if it wasn't cheap
10 I'd worry less about my health

11 a
2 I'll go on holiday next summer if ...
3 I'll speak to my mother next week if ...
4 If I won the lottery, I'd ...
5 I'll go to bed early tonight if ...
6 I'd stop studying English if ...

12 a
1 Paola and Jayne
2 Miko, Roger and Jaime
3 Tomas, Miko and Jayne
4 Miko
b
1 T
2 F
3 T
4 F
5 T
6 F

13 2 wealthy
3 education
4 homelessness
5 healthcare
6 unemployment
7 taxpayers
8 corruption
9 racism
10 poor

14 2 the opposition parties
3 defence
4 waste money on
5 healthcare
6 corruption
7 reduce taxes for
8 taxpayers'
9 Unemployment
10 racism
11 the wealthy
12 pollution

Answer key

UNIT 11

1 **a**
2 You're allowed to walk on the grass.
3 Are we allowed to use a calculator?
4 Visitors are not allowed to touch the exhibits.
5 On Saturdays, we're allowed to stay up until ten o'clock.
6 Children under five are not allowed to use the swimming pool without an adult.
7 Am I allowed to hang pictures on the walls?
8 You're allowed to wear casual clothes.
9 You aren't allowed to use your mobile phone in here.
10 Are we allowed to take photos in here?
b
2 can
3 aren't allowed to
4 must
5 shouldn't
6 don't have to
7 mustn't
8 ought to
9 can't
10 are allowed to

2 **a**
2 should
3 aren't allowed
4 are allowed
5 can't
6 ought
7 don't have
8 mustn't
9 can
10 must

3 2 SC, Can I book aerobics classes in advance?
3 LIB, How long am I allowed to keep books?
4 LC, Do I have to take a test?
5 SC, Should I bring a photo?
6 LC, How many classes am I allowed to miss?

4 **a**
2 Students mustn't arrive late.
3 You ought to talk to her about it.
4 We have to be there 30 minutes before it starts.
5 I'm not allowed to copy this text.
6 You shouldn't say things like that.
7 You don't have to wear jeans, but you can if you want to.
8 You can't use your phone in here.

5 2 as a result
3 What is more
4 Despite this
5 although
6 for this reason
7 Besides
8 therefore

6 2 c
3 a
4 a
5 c
6 b
7 b

7 2 I had to clean my boots everyday.
3 I wasn't allowed to have long hair.
4 I couldn't email home.
5 We could watch a movie every Saturday evening.
6 We were allowed to go into town once a month.
7 I didn't have to pay for my meals.

8 A
2 No, we weren't.
3 How many questions did you have to answer?
4 We had to do twenty in three hours.
B
1 Were you allowed to stay up late?
2 Yeah, we could sit by the campfire until midnight.
3 Did you have to get up early?
4 No, we didn't have to get up until nine.
C
1 Did Francoise have a good time in Australia?
2 No, she had to work six days a week.
3 That's terrible!
4 And she wasn't allowed to phone us.

9 2 don't have to
3 had to
4 have to
5 didn't have to
6 don't have to
7 mustn't
8 must

10 **a**
1 Mario Silva
2 Fernando Silva
3 Lisa Stowe
4 Beatrice
5 Mario Silva
6 Dominique Moceneau
7 Dumitru Moceneau, Lisa Stowe
8 Beatrice, Dominique Moceneau
b
1 c
2 e
3 a
4 b
5 d

11 **a**
2 I don't know about that. In my opinion
3 I take your point; to be honest I don't really agree
4 What do you mean?
5 You have to remember that
6 I don't know about you, but I think

12 **a**
1C 2A 3B
b
2 mean
3 In
4 about
5 don't
6 but
7 take
8 honest
c
1B 2C 3A

13 2 to meet
3 It is often used
4 that it should
5 have done
6 Firstly,
7 criminals who have
8 What is more,
9 For that reason,
10 important arguments
11 people
12 to commit
13 unnecessary
14 justice is a
15 from repeating

UNIT 12

1 1 F, 2 D, 3 B, 4 E, 4 E, 5 A, 6 C

3
2 could have eaten your sandwich
3 could have left your wallet in the bank
4 could have caught an earlier train
5 They could have gone to the wrong place to meet us.
6 I could have been out when you called.
7 Dave could have got stuck in traffic.
8 You could have left the caps lock key on.

3
2 You shouldn't have told Tom (my secret).
3 We should have taken a taxi.
4 You should have discussed it with me first.
5 He shouldn't have left it in his car.
6 Someone should have told me that Gerard was a vegetarian.
7 I shouldn't have stayed out late last night.
8 He should have studied (for his exam).

5
2 You shouldn't **have** taken her book without asking first.
3 They still haven't confirmed delivery. **Could we** have sent it to the wrong address?
4 Rio really shouldn't have **given** up football. He was so talented.
5 I wouldn't have **stopped** to break up the fight like Mike did. It was too dangerous.
6 Fatih and Vera **couldn't** have known about the party, or they would have come.
7 I know I should have **called** you sooner, but I've been so busy.
8 Thanks for all your help, I **couldn't** have done it without you.
9 In your position, I would **have** backed up my files first.
10 The doctor should have **told** you sooner.

6
2 would have liked
3 couldn't have run
4 shouldn't have listened
5 should have done
6 could have had
7 wouldn't have believed
8 could have been
9 would have bought

7 **a**
2 could walk
3 wouldn't have stayed
4 could have invited
5 shouldn't have turned
6 I would have bought

8 2 h, 3 d, 4 a, 5 g, 6 b, 7 e, 8 f

9
2 wouldn't be
3 have arrived
4 have picked you up
5 hadn't
6 hadn't missed
7 would have won
8 had cast
9 hadn't walked
10 be

10 **a**
1 He ran away from home because his parents forced him to enrol in an electrician's course and because he wanted 'to become something in life'.
2 His family thought he was dead.

b
2 If he hadn't run away he would have done an electrician's course.
3 If he'd stayed at home, he'd be an electrician now.
4 He wouldn't have had enough money to study if he hadn't worked as a waiter.
5 If he had written to his parents, they wouldn't have thought he was dead.
6 If they hadn't seen the programme they would have still thought he was dead.
7 He wouldn't have scored 86.5 percent if he hadn't worked hard.
8 If he hadn't been very clever, he wouldn't have won the award.

11 2 f, 3 e, 4 a, 5 g, 6 h, 7 b, 8 d

12 **a**
1 C
2 A
3 B

2
1 A Casablanca
  B on the ship, the Titanic
  C in Russia
2 A Rick Blaine, Ilsa, Victor
  B Rose, Jack, the rich fiancé
  C the doctor, his wife and his lover
3 A sad
  B sad
  C both

13 **a**
2 paid
3 received
4 dates
5 booking
6 sent
7 heard
8 write

b
correct order: f, c, a, h, b, e, g, d

Pearson Education Limited
Edinburgh Gate
Harlow
Essex CM20 2JE
England
and Associated Companies throughout the world.

www.pearsonelt.com

© Pearson Education Limited 2013

The right of Jane Comyns Carr, Frances Eales and Damian Williams to be identified as authors of this Work has been asserted by them in accordance with the Copyright, Designs and Patents Act 1988.

All rights reserved; no part of this publication may be reproduced, stored in a retrieval system, or transmitted in any form or by any means, electronic, mechanical, photocopying, recording, or otherwise without the prior written permission of the Publishers.

Under no circumstances may any part of this book be photocopied for resale.

First published 2013

ISBN: 978-1-4479-0652-0

Set in 10.5pt Bless Light
Printed in Slovakia by Neografia

Acknowledgements
We are grateful to the following for permission to reproduce copyright material:
Logos
Logo on page 52 from eBay Inc., www.ebay.com. Reproduced by permission. eBay Logo is a trademark of eBay Inc.
Text
Extract on page 13 from Matt Connolley for extracts from www.iusedtobelieve.com. Reproduced with permission; Extract on page 24 adapted from British Sky Broadcasting Ltd for an extract adapted from "Johnny Depp", www.skymovies.com. Reproduced with permission; Extracts on page 44 adapted from Customer Reviews, copyright © Amazon.com, Inc. All rights reserved. Used with permission; Extract on page 73 adapted from 'Missing Indian boy spotted on TV winning exams award', 12 June 2003, originally published on www.ananova.com, copyright © Orange Digital Ltd; Extract on page 81 from eBay Inc. mission statement, www.ebay.com. Reproduced by permission.

In some instances we have been unable to trace the owners of copyright material, and we would appreciate any information that would enable us to do so.

Photo acknowledgements
The publisher would like to thank the following for their kind permission to reproduce their photographs:

(Key: b-bottom; c-centre; l-left; r-right; t-top)

Alamy Images: Bananastock 64, David Fleetham 19, Steve Mansfield-Devine 18t; **Corbis:** Kim Steele / Blend Images 49l; **Fotolia.com:** AlexQ 18c, Matthew Antonino 32tl, Arctos 34, Arvind Balaraman 73, Galina Barskaya 56, Beboy 21t, corepics 46, Sandra Cunningham 67b, eurobanks 32tr, Mat Hayward 32bl, imageegami 51, JackF 71, MasterLu 21b, Misha 65, Monart Design 5, Monkey Business 40, Lynne Nicholson 58, Darren Pellegrino 17, wajan 72, WavebreakMediaMicro 60bl; **Pearson Education Ltd:** Gareth Boden 10; **PhotoDisc:** Karl Weatherly 60br; **Press Association Images:** HT / ABACA USA / Empics Entertainment 24, PBG / PBG / Empics Entertainment 44b; **Rex Features:** Moviestore Collection 44tl, SNAP 44tr; **Shutterstock.com:** Andreea S 36, Yuri Arcurs 32br, 35b, Antonio Diaz 67t, Elena Elisseeva 62, Goodluz 25, grynold 63, Netfalls – Remy Musser 35c, nmedia 16, Diana Taliun 50, Max Topchii 9, Phil Tragen 8, Vovan 50t; **SuperStock:** Andrew Michael / age fotostock 4, AsiaPix 49r, Corbis 31; **The Kobal Collection:** 20th Century Fox / Paramount 74

Cover images: *Front:* **Shutterstock.com:** Rodho

All other images © Pearson Education

In some instances we have been unable to trace the owners of copyright material, and we would appreciate any information that would enable us to do so.

Illustrated by Kathy Baxendale, Colin Brown, Joan Corlass, Nicky Dupays, Stephanie Hawken, Conny Jude, Tim Kahane, Aziz Khan, Ian Mitchell, Julian Mosedale, Nicky Taylor and Teresa Tibberts